The Wicca Garden

Also by Gerina Dunwich

Candlelight Spells
Wicca Candle Magick
The Concise Lexicon of the Occult
Wicca Craft
Wicca Love Spells
The Wicca Spellbook
The Wicca Book of Days
Circle of Shadows (poetry)
Words of the Cosmic Winds (poetry)

The Wicca Garden

A Modern Witch's Book of Magickal and Enchanted Herbs and Plants

Gerina Dunwich

Citadel Press
Kensington Publishing Corp.
www.kensingtonbooks.com

This book is dedicated to my Gemini soul mate,
Al Jackter; my mother; and Wilva.
Goddess bless you.

CITADEL PRESS books are published by

Kensington Publishing Corp.
850 Third Avenue
New York, NY 10022

Copyright © 1996 Gerina Dunwich

All Kensington titles, imprints, and distributed lines are available at special quantity discounts for bulk purchases for sales promotions, premiums, fund raising, educational, or institutional use. Special book excerpts or customized printings can also be created to fit specific needs. For details, write or phone the office of the Kensington special sales manager: Kensington Publishing Corp., 850 Third Avenue, New York, NY 10022, attn: Special Sales Department, phone 1-800-221-2647.

Citadel Press logo Reg. U.S. Patent and Trademark Office
Citadel Press is a trademark of Kensington Publishing Corp.

First printing 1996

10 9 8 7 6 5 4

Printed in the United States of America

Library of Congress Cataloging-in-Publication Data

Dunwich, Gerina
    The Wicca garden : a modern witch's book of magickal and enchanted
    herbs and plants / Gerina Dunwich.
        p.   cm.
    "A Citadel Press Book."
    Includes bibliographical references and index.
    ISBN 0-8065-1777-8 (pbk.)
    1. Witchcraft.   2. Plants—Miscellanea.   3. Herbs—Miscellanea.
    4. Magic   I. Title.
BF1572.P43D86   1996
133.4'3—dc20   95–47086
                                                          CIP

Contents

Introduction

Welcome, my friends, to the Wicca Garden. It is an enchanted world of green magick where flowers and trees possess the power to heal the sick as well as to bewitch. It is also a mysterious place of superstition, omens, and ancient folklore.

For those of you who are unfamiliar with Wicca, I will try to explain it with a brief excerpt from the introduction to my book *Wicca Craft*: "Wicca (an alternative name for modern Witchcraft) is a positive, shamanistic, nature religion with two main deities honored and worshipped in Wiccan rites: the Goddess (the female aspect and a deity related to the ancient Mother Goddess in Her triple aspect of Maiden, Mother, and Crone) and Her consort, the Horned God (the male aspect).

Wicca often includes the practice of various forms of white magick (usually for healing purposes or as a counter to negativity) as well as rites to attune oneself with the natural rhythm of life forces marked by the phases of the moon and the four seasons."

For additional information about the ways of Wicca (which is also known as "the Craft of the Wise" or often just "the Craft"), please read my other books *Wicca Craft* and *The Wicca Spellbook*.

The art of wortcunning (the use of and knowledge of the secret healing and magickal properties of herbs) is a very important facet of the Wicca Craft, and the relationship between herbs and the Craft goes back a long, long way.

"Herbal sorcery" was a renowned art in ancient times

(especially in the mythology-rich country of Greece). Medicinal gardens were common, and all plants and trees were believed to be governed by the gods and goddesses whose hands guided the destiny of man.

In medieval times, Witches experimented with wild-growing plants, and it was not long before they learned of the wonderful, magickal healing qualities found in many flowers, roots, and leaves.

The power to heal wounds and to cure the ills of both man and beast soon became the Witch's trademark, and many wise old women were hanged or burned because they possessed knowledge which was forbidden by the Christian Church.

In modern times, many Witches continue to grow and use nature's herbal remedies to combat illness and disease. Wortcunning is a talent that seems to come naturally to many in the Craft, and most country-dwelling Wiccans (and many city ones as well) are skilled in the art of preparing healing herbal potions.

However, the curative power of plants and trees is not limited by any means to potions alone. Herbs are also used in sachets, amulets, and homemade candles crafted especially for healing spells and rituals. (Even store-bought candles can be charged with healing herb power by being anointed with an oil made from the appropriate herb.)

In addition to healing, all blossoms, leaves, roots, thorns, bark, and seeds have long been employed by women and men of the Craft for divinational purposes. Botanomancy (the art and practice of divination by herbs) has been practiced since ancient times by nearly every culture around the world.

Over the course of time, numerous methods of drawing omens from plants have been devised, from the simple tossing of sticks, seeds, or flower petals to spell out messages, to the reading of tea leaves (also known as "tasseography"), to the burning of herbs and then interpreting the flames, odor, crackle, color, or shape and direction of the smoke produced.

Herbal divination has been used to foretell future events, identify the guilty, and discover that which is unknown or hidden.

Magick is a powerful tool and an important skill to many who follow the path of Wicca. And where would the magickal arts be without herbs for love philtres, wands, natural amulets, incense, oils, sachets, candle scents, and so forth?

A word of caution: Although the Wicca Garden is a wondrous place of healing power, magick, and love, like everything else, it does have a dark side which should be approached only with the utmost caution.

Many folks have been made seriously ill by experimenting with potent medicinal herbs or by deliberately abusing potentially dangerous plants for their intoxicating or hallucinogenic properties. Some have even been poisoned to death.

With this in mind, you should *never* attempt to gather wild herbs for medicinal use unless you are an herb expert or are accompanied by someone who is a trained, experienced herbalist. Also, do not rely on illustrations in books to determine which herbs are safe to use and which are dangerous. Many poisonous and nonpoisonous plants possess identical features which can easily be confused.

There are also some very noxious weeds out there with evil properties employed by those foolish enough to follow the left-hand path (black magick). Their nasty uses are outlined in many grimoires, especially those written in the Middle Ages.

Using such plants to hex your enemies in any way is not consistent with the positive, loving ways of Wicca. In fact, using any form of black magick for any reason is generally frowned upon in all circles of the Wicca Craft, for it is a violation of the Wiccan Rede which states: "An it harm none, do what thou wilt."

If you practice magick with deliberate, evil intent, you are headed for self-destruction, because whatever evil power you send out to others is soon returned to you three times as strong. (The same also applies to good power.) This threefold karmic retribution is known as the Threefold Law (or Law of Three), and trust me when I tell you that it works every time you do something good or bad, even if you do not believe that it will. So always think twice before you cast a spell, and make it a point to use magick in a positive and constructive fashion.

Whether you are an initiated Priestess/Priest or a novice Witch, a covener or a solitary, I hope this book will help guide you on your spiritual journey to Light and Love.

The Wicca Garden is a sacred garden of the Goddess and the Horned God, and all are welcome to stroll down its meandering, moss-covered path. It is a place of beauty and dreams. It is a realm where wisdom grows and magick is always in bloom.

BLESSED BE!

The Wicca Garden

1

Herb Gardening

Many Wiccans and modern Witches enjoy growing their own herbs, whether they be in a small garden in the backyard, an herb farm, or just a few flowerpots on a sunny windowsill in the kitchen.

Homegrown herbs offer the Witch-gardener .many benefits. In the long run, they are less expensive than herbs sold in occult shops and Witchcraft supply catalogues. They are especially potent in spellcasting and magickal work, and the pleasure and feeling of accomplishment that is experienced by watching a seed planted by your own hands grown into a beautiful mature plant is a special reward.

Throughout the years, wortcunning has played an important role in the Craft of the Wise.

Witches have grown their own herbs since ancient times, and they were the first ones to discover and put to use the healing power of many plants, long before medicine or modern science as we now know it existed.

In nearly every country village, there was at least one wise old Witchy-woman skilled in the arts of magick and herbalism, who could remedy just about any malady of human or beast with an herbal potion, poultice, or charm bag filled with special roots, flowers, and other magickal things.

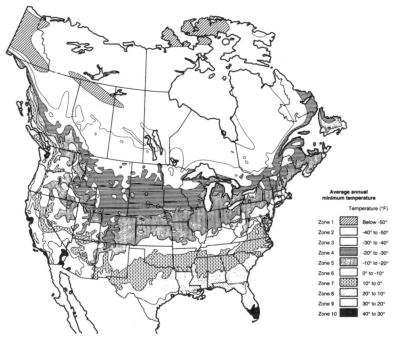

United States Dept. of Agriculture Plant Hardiness Zone Map

Most herbs prefer to grow in a sunny location. There are a handful that grow well in heavy shade, and some that can tolerate partial shade. (These are discussed later in this chapter.)

If the herb you intend to grow is not included in the list of shade herbs, you should plant it in a spot where it will receive five or six hours of full sun each day.

To prevent later uprooting or damage, be sure that the spot you choose is sheltered from the wind. A strong gust can flatten a young, delicate plant or even rip it completely out of the ground.

Good soil and good drainage are essential for the success of most plants, and most are happiest in a neutral or slightly alkaline soil. A pH factor of 6 to 7.5 is ideal.

The phase of the Moon and the sign of the zodiac the Moon is in when the herb is planted are extremely important, as favorable results are always obtained when plants are planted in harmony with Mother Nature.

According to the centuries-old rule of lunar gardening, most herbs should be planted during a new or waxing Moon in the astrological sign of Cancer, Scorpio, or Pisces.

The exceptions to the rule are as follows: Garlic should be planted during a new or waxing Moon in the sign of Scorpio or Sagittarius. Parsley (which is extremely slow to germinate) should be planted during a new Moon in the sign of Pisces, Cancer, Libra, or Scorpio. Root crops should be planted during a waxing or full Moon in the sign of Taurus. Sage should be planted during a full Moon in the sign of Pisces, Scorpio, or Cancer. Valerian should be planted during a new or waxing Moon in the sign of Gemini or Virgo. Vines and flowers should be planted during a new or waxing Moon in the sign of Libra.

The following signs of the zodiac are considered the Fruitful Signs: Cancer, Scorpio, Pisces, Taurus, Capricorn, and Libra (which is the least beneficial of these signs).

The following signs of the zodiac are considered the

Barren Signs: Leo, Gemini, Virgo, Sagittarius, Aquarius, and Aries.

With the exception of garlic and valerian, herbs should never be planted when the Moon is positioned in one of the Barren Signs of the zodiac. Also, under no circumstances should you ever plant, transplant, bud, or graft during the waning phase of the Moon.

Herbs can be grown from root divisions, layered stems, and so on; however, annuals are the quickest and easiest plants to grow from seed. Nursery-grown plants are another option to consider if you prefer an instant garden and don't mind spending a little more money.

For a healthy garden, do not overwater, and be sure to keep the area free of weeds, which not only make a garden look unattractive but also compete with cultivated plants for nutrients and water. If weeds are not controlled regularly, they will spread and eventually "choke" the garden.

Weeds (as well as garden pests) should be destroyed when the waning Moon is positioned in the Barren Sign of Leo, Virgo, Aquarius, or Aries.

Chemical weedkillers are dangerous and definitely not recommended for use in herb or vegetable gardens. Mulches, black plastic sheeting, and good old-fashioned weed pulling are the best methods of weed control.

Dandelions and most of the common nonpoisonous weeds are said to be high in vitamins and are very nutritious. They must be harvested when young, and one most certainly has to learn to acquire a taste for them. (Please note: *Never* eat any plant if you are unsure of its safety!)

Plowing and cultivation of the soil should begin when the waning Moon is in any of the Barren Signs.

Compost should be started when the waning Moon is in the sign of Cancer, Pisces, or Scorpio.

The best time for fertilizing or transplanting is when the waxing Moon is in the sign of Cancer, Pisces, or Scorpio.

To encourage more bushy growth of herbs, harvest the leaves and pinch out flowering shoots. Pruning to encourage growth and bud development should be done when the Moon is in the Fruitful Sign of Cancer, Scorpio, or Capricorn.

Pruning to discourage growth should be done when the Moon is in the Barren Sign of Sagittarius or Aries.

Harvesting herbs for drying should be done on a dry day after the morning dew has evaporated and before the sun is at its height.

Gather herbs and roots for storage when the Moon is in the Barren Sign of Gemini, Aquarius, or Aries.

A Witch's Garden Spell

To empower your new herb garden with magickal energy and to protect it against all evil and negative influences, perform the following garden spell after planting your garden:

Place a small cauldron or goblet down on the center of an altar. Fill it with water and place one green candle to the left of the water, and another one to the right. Light the left candle first and then use its flame to light the right one.

Pick up your consecrated athame (Witch's ritual knife with a double-edged blade). Holding it with its blade down and its handle between your palms in a traditional prayer position, dip the blade into the water.

Visualize the water being magickally charged with

Goddess energy in the form of white light emanating from the tip of the athame's blade.

As you do this, repeat the following magickal rhyme:

> God and Goddess, hear my verse,
> Let this water be free of curse.
> Bless it with the love of Thine
> O Ancient Pagan Ones divine.

Return the athame to the altar and extinguish the flames of the two green candles. The first half of the spell is complete.

Pour the magickally charged water from the cauldron or goblet into a watering can and immediately go outside and water your garden with it as you repeat the following magickal rhyme:

> With black Mother Earth
> With golden fire Sun
> With life-giving water
> This spell's begun.
>
> Wiccan garden, root and flower,
> I charge thee now with magick power.
> Seeds sown by these hands of mine
> Grow into herbs to heal and divine.
>
> Elemental spirits hearken:
> I ask thee now protect this garden.
> Keep it safe from storm and foe
> So Witches' herbs can sprout and grow.
>
> Garden spell, now work for me.
> This is my will. So mote it be!

Drying Herbs

There are many methods, both old and new, of drying herbs.

In olden days, herbs were spread out on the floor of the attic, where the air was warm and dry. In about two weeks, they would be dry. If the weather was humid, the drying time would take a little longer.

Herbs can also be dried by placing them on muslin-covered racks or by hanging them upside down in a north-facing window or in a warm and well-ventilated place such as over a radiator, where the drying process will take from two to eight days.

You can also dry your herbs quickly in a gas or electric oven turned on to the lowest temperature setting. Spread the herbs out on an ungreased cookie sheet and place in the oven for five to ten minutes, or until the herbs become dry to the touch. Keep the oven door open while the herbs are being dried in order to permit the moisture to escape. Do not overbake the herbs, or they will lose the oils which give them their distinctive flavors and aromas.

A modern Witch's method of drying herbs is to spread the leaves out on a paper towel and then place it in a microwave oven on high for no more than two minutes.

After the herbs have been dried by whichever method you have chosen, hang the leaves in bunches in a closet to use later in potpourris, to season food, and so forth. Or, if you prefer, you can gently crumble the dried herbs between your fingertips and place them in jars with seals that are airtight. (Note: I do not recommend that you crumble bay leaves. For best culinary results, they should be stored whole.) Be sure to discard the stems, as they have a tendency to retain a bit of moisture, which later can produce mold on the herbs while in storage.

A sixteenth-century herb garden.

Shade Herbs

Some herbs, especially woodland perennials, can grow quite well in a heavily shaded herb bed. These include bistort, bugle, deadly nightshade, evening primrose, goldenseal, hellebore, lily of the valley, lungwort, mandrake (European), pennyroyal, ramsons, Solomon's seal, sweet violet, valerian, and woodruff.

Herbs that can grow in partial shade are abscess root, angelica, birthroot, figwort, foxglove, greater celandine, ground ivy, Jacob's ladder, lady's mantle, monkshood, spignel, sweet cicely, wild strawberry, wintergreen, wood avens, and wood sage.

Herbs that can tolerate some shade include alexanders, black horehound, burdock, chervil, chives, comfrey, garden sorrel, goat's rue, Good King Henry, henbane, honeysuckle, lady's bedstraw, lemon balm, madder, marsh mallow, meadow saffron, mints, musk mallow, parsley, pellitory of the wall, poke root, primrose, purslane, rocket, Saint John's wort, teazel, and wild celery.

Herbs for Ponds, Rivers, and Marshlands

Herbs that grow wild in marshlands and along the banks of rivers are angelica, birthroot, bistort, bloodroot, bogbean, bog myrtle, comfrey, elecampane, fleabane, garden sorrel, goldenseal, gravel root, hemp agrimony, Indian physic, Jacob's ladder, mace, marsh mallow, meadowsweet, skullcap, sneezewort, soapwort, sweet cicely, sweet flag, valerian, watercress, water figwort, and water mint.

If your herb garden has a shallow pond, you should consider planting bogbean, sweet flag, or yellow flag. These are three herbs that grow especially well near water.

If the soil in your garden contains a large amount of heavy, damp clay, plant comfrey or elecampane, which are two of the most tolerant of herbs. They are large plants that grow in spreading clumps.

The Indoor Herb Garden

If you choose to grow your herbs indoors in flowerpots, troughs, or boxes, it is important to bear in mind that they will need at least a half a day of sunlight.

Keep them on a sunny windowsill facing south in a room that is airy and somewhat humid, if at all possible.

Bay, lemon balm, and mints need only partial sun when grown indoors and can be placed in windows with an eastern or western exposure.

Indoor plants can also be grown under artificial light if you do not have windows with the proper exposure. (Fourteen to sixteen hours of fluorescent light exposure daily is necessary if it is the plant's only source of light; otherwise, three hours of fluorescent light exposure daily to supplement natural sunlight should be sufficient.)

The worst place to put potted herbs is on or directly above a radiator. The hot and dry atmosphere produced by the heater will cause plants to dehydrate and die.

A small kitchen filled with cooking fumes and fluctuating heat is also not a suitable place. Sudden temperature changes will have a negative effect on your plants.

Be sure to use pots deep enough for the plant's roots to grow (at least eight inches). Cover the bottom of the pot with pebbles or marbles to permit adequate drainage, and always use potting soil, as it contains more nutrients than ordinary dirt from the backyard.

Be careful not to overwater your indoor plants. Moisten (not saturate) the soil with lukewarm or room temperature water once or twice a week. Morning is the ideal time to water. Afternoon and evening watering often results in fungus and rot developing on the roots and stems of plants.

The following culinary herbs can be grown indoors as

houseplants: apple mint, balm, burnet, chervil, chicory, costmary, dill, dittany of Crete, geraniums, Good King Henry, Johnny-jump-up, lemon verbena, myrtle, nasturtium, parsley, purple basil, rosemary, samphire, summer savory, sweet basil, sweet bay, sweet marjoram, sweet violet, tarragon, white mustard, winter savory, and woodruff.

Halloween Pumpkins

The carving of Halloween pumpkins, also know as jack-o'-lanterns, is a very old Pagan custom which dates back to the days of the ancient Druids.

They believed that on Samhain Eve (October 31) the spirits of the dead returned to the world of the living for one night. Many of these disembodied spirits were the ghosts of deceased family members, friends, and ancestors who were allowed to leave the world of the dead to rejoice with their living loved ones. However, some of the ghosts who walked among the living on this dark and magickal night were believed to be of an evil nature and were greatly feared. Some were the vengeful ghosts of sorcerers, and some were evil specters who took delight in devouring the souls of humans.

For protection, jack-o'-lanterns with hideous candlelit faces were carved out of pumpkins and carried as lanterns from house to house to scare away the malevolent spirits.

In modern times, the jack-o'-lantern is an important symbol of the Samhain Eve Witches' Sabbat (which is also know as Halloween).

It is traditionally carved with a white-handled knife known as an athame, and lit when the first shadows of night fall, to honor the spirits of deceased loved ones.

The jack-o'-lantern also serves as a tool of divination

and a symbolic fire to light the way for the Witches' New Year. And, of course, pumpkin pie is one of the traditional Sabbat foods of Samhain.

Many non-Pagans, unaware of the jack-o'-lantern's Pagan origin and religious functions, put a carved pumpkin on their front porch or in a window each year on Halloween simply as a spooky decoration to amuse the neighborhood trick-or-treaters.

Pumpkins are often expensive to buy in city supermarkets, and inexpensive in the country at farm stands and private homes. Many Wiccans with enough room in their gardens prefer to grow their own pumpkins for Samhain Eve.

If you decide to grow your own pumpkins, here are some important gardening tips you should follow: Pumpkins grow best in full sun and in soil that is fertile and moisture holding. After any danger of frost has passed, seeds should be planted about an inch deep in the ground. Be sure to space each plant approximately four to eight feet apart for small pumpkins, and eight to twelve feet apart for large varieties, on hills in rows spaced eight feet apart. According to the rules of lunar gardening, pumpkins should be planted when the waxing Moon is positioned in a Fruitful Sign (Cancer, Scorpio, Pisces, Taurus, Capricorn, or Libra).

Dust for striped beetle and water the plants frequently unless you live in an area with adequate rainfall.

Allow the entire plant to grow; however, you should cut off extra fruits, leaving only one or two on each plant.

Growing pumpkins generally require a large gardening space (approximately thirty-six feet by sixteen feet for about ten pumpkins). However, there are a few varieties of pumpkins (such as the "Cinderella") that require only six feet per plant.

The Pentagram Garden

Choose a level site in a sunny location for your pentagram herb garden.

Drive a stake into the ground where you wish the center of the garden to be. Tie one end of a string to the stake, and the other end to a bottle filled with sand. (Use a string four feet long if you are making a pentagram garden with a diameter of eight feet; three feet of string for one with a diameter of six feet, and so forth.)

With string taut, turn the bottle upside down, allowing the sand to slowly pour out as you walk clockwise in a complete circle. The sand will mark the outer circle of the pentagram, which you can then cover with bricks, stones, seashells, etc.

Remove the stake, string and bottle, and then prepare the soil within the circle.

Using the edge of a board as a guide, lay down five straight lines of bricks or stones inside the circle to form a symbol of the five-pointed star.

Once the pentagram outline is complete, you can then begin planting herbs in the garden. To add even more interest to it, plant different species of herbs in each section of the pentagram and put a small sundial, birdbath, Goddess statue, or other garden decoration in the center. If the pentagram is outlined with bricks, use paint or chalk to decorate them with magickal and astrological symbols.

Garlic (*Allium sativum*)

Garlic, which is ruled by the planet Mars, and under the astrological influence of Aries and Scorpio, has been reputed since ancient Egyptian times to bestow physical strength upon those who eat it.

As an herb of the magickal arts, garlic is used in exorcisms, purification rites, and for protection against evil influences. According to old European folklore, garlic also possesses the supernatural power to keep blood-drinking vampires at bay.

To grow your own garlic, plant garlic cloves (pointed end up with skin intact) in the spring or in the fall. If you choose to plant in the fall, it should be done in the month of October when the new or first-quarter Moon is in the astrological sign of Scorpio or Sagittarius. However, if you live in an area of the country where the soil freezes in the winter, I recommend that you plant it in the spring when the Moon is in the same phase and astrological sign as just mentioned.

A good-sized garlic bulb bought at the local supermarket should yield enough cloves to start approximately a dozen garlic plants.

Garlic likes to grow in friable rich soil and full sun, and will need plenty of compost, manure, and water to make it healthy and happy.

Space each garlic clove four to six inches apart in moist soil. Keep their tops half an inch below the surface of the ground. Plant seeds only one-fourth of an inch deep.

You can grow garlic as a perennial if you live in a region with mild winters and if you use proper winter cover.

A garlic plant has sparse, flat leaves and grows to be about eighteen inches high. A small cluster of pink or white flowers blooms at the top of the plant's stalk from the beginning of the summer season throughout July.

In midsummer, when the color of the garlic's leaves change to yellow, dig up the plant and cure the compound bulb by placing it in a dark and dry place for several weeks before storing.

Garlic has been used medicinally for hundreds of years, possessing both antiseptic and antibiotic properties which have been confirmed by numerous modern studies.

2

Herbs of Magick

Herbs of Wiccan Dreamcraft

To bring restful sleep and pleasant dreams, prepare a tea from white wine and the herb known as lesser celandine. Use a spoonful of honey or sugar to sweeten it and then drink it before retiring for the evening.

In addition to, or in place of, the tea, you can place any of the following magickal dream herbs underneath or sew inside your pillow: catnip, hops, mistletoe, passionflower leaves, psyllium seeds, or vervain.

Rubbing the juice of a lettuce on your forehead or eating its leaves before going to sleep will also help to promote sweet dreams and a good night's rest.

For spiritual protection while sleeping, burn cedar incense in your bedroom before going to bed; keep a live hyacinth plant near your bed; or sleep with any of the following herbs underneath your pillow: anise seeds, marigold flowers, mistletoe, mullein, purslane, rosemary, thyme, Ti plant, or yarrow. These protective magickal herbs will also guard a sleeper against nightmares, psychic attacks, and baleful phantoms of the night.

To facilitate dreams with guidance for love matters, sleep with any of the following herbs above your bed or underneath your pillow: cinquefoil, marjoram, vervain, or yarrow.

To help bring on spiritual guidance dreams, drink a mint tea before retiring for the evening, or sleep with either Buchu leaves or mint leaves underneath your pillow.

Mugwort, one of the most potent herbs of dreamcraft, aids in astral projection and lucid dreaming when burned as a magickal incense or placed underneath a pillow prior to sleeping.

Many Witches who practice the art of dreamcraft brew a magickal tea-potion from mugwort and drink it just before going to bed in order to strengthen their psychic and magickal dream powers.

The following herbs have been used by Witches and spiritual dreamworkers since ancient times to enhance dream recall: mugwort, passionflower leaves, and rosemary. Drink any of the three as a magickal tea-potion just before going to bed or sleep with one of them underneath your pillow.

To facilitate dream divination and enhance dreams with insights into the future, burn frankincense, dried jasmine flowers, or mugwort as a magickal incense in your bedroom before going to sleep.

A tea-potion brewed from mugwort or rosebuds will also work well, as will sleeping with any of the following herbs over or underneath your bed: ash leaves, bay leaves, cinquefoil, heliotrope, holly, jasmine flowers, marigold flowers, mimosa, mugwort, onion, or yarrow.

The following herbs have been traditionally used by Wiccans and modern Witches in magickal dream pillows and potions to induce prophetic dream visions: adder's tongue, agrimony, anise, camphor, cinnamon, daisy, holly, hops, ivy, lemon verbena, lesser celandine, mandrake root, marigold, mistletoe, mugwort, onion, peppermint, purslane, rose, Saint John's wort, verbena, vervain, wormwood, and yarrow.

To promote healing dreams, drink a tca-potion made from catnip or mint; burn cedar as a magickal dream incense; or sleep with agrimony, catnip, mint, sandalwood or thyme underneath your pillow.

To bring on dreams that facilitate spiritual/psychic growth, burn frankincense or mugwort as a magickal incense in your bedroom prior to sleeping, drink mugwort tea, or sleep with the herb underneath or sewn into your pillow.

The Evil Eye

The evil eye is the inborn supernatural power to cause bewitchment, harm, misfortune, or death to others (human or animal) by an angry or venomous glare.

According to folklore, some people are naturally born with this power; others acquire it only after signing their names in blood in the Devil's infamous black book and promising their souls to him upon the moment of their deaths.

Over the centuries, the superstitious from all corners of the globe have devised various methods to detect, protect against, and destroy the evil eye. Many of these methods included the amuletic use of certain roots, flowers, seeds, leaves, barks, and berries that were believed to possess magickal or divine powers to combat the evil eye.

The following herbs have been traditionally used by Witches and shamans in spells, ointments, mojo bags, and poppets to ward off the evil eye or to counteract curses brought on by it: anise leaves, castor beans, figwort, garlic, henna, hyacinth, lady's slipper, lavender, lime tree twigs, pennyroyal, periwinkle, and tulip.

In Russia the birch tree is believed to offer magickal protection against the evil eye when red ribbons are tied to its branches.

In ancient Rome, rue was eaten to ward off the evil eye, and small horns filled with sage were worn on necklaces as amuletic jewelry for protection.

Herbs Associated With Astral Projection

Dittany of Crete aids out-of-body experiences when mixed with equal parts of benzoin, sandalwood, and vanilla and burned as a magickal incense prior to astral projection.

Mugwort, a popular Witches' herb, can also aid in achieving astral projection when it is placed inside a magick dream pillow.

In the Middle Ages, poplar leaves were used by Witches as an ingredient in their notorious flying ointments. If rubbed on the body or placed under your pillow prior to sleeping, the leaves and buds of the poplar are said to open the gateway between the physical world and the astral plane.

Witches' Herbs From A to Z

The following is an alphabetical listing of many significant herbs (including trees) associated with Wicca and the magickal arts, along with their magickal properties.

Many of the herbs (especially poisonous ones) used by Witches in ancient times are no longer used in present-day Witchcraft; however, they are included in this section for their historical value.

ACACIA

The acacia is any of various tropical trees of Africa belonging to the genus *Acacia*, having clusters of white or yellow flowers and yielding a gum. Its sprigs and bark have been used magickally by Witches to attract money, inspire love, ward off evil, and enhance the psychic powers. Acacia is one of the traditional ritual herbs of the Lammas Sabbat.

ACONITE

Also known by the folk names "wolfbane" and "monkshood," aconite was used in flying ointments of the Middle Ages. It was mixed with belladonna and fat (along with a variety of other vile ingredients) and then rubbed on the body to produce the sensation of flying through the air. Practitioners of sorcery used its toxic juices as a "Witches' poison" to do away with enemies and rivals. Aconite was used throughout Europe as an herbal amulet for protection against werewolves and vampires. Its seeds have been used by magicians to magickally master the powers of invisibility.

ADDER'S TONGUE

The adder's tongue is a Witches' herb of healing. It is also used as a magickal herb of divination, dream magick, and lunar magick. Also known by the folk name "dogtooth violet," the adder's tongue is a sacred flower of all serpent-goddesses.

AFRICAN VIOLET

As an herb of the magickal arts, the African violet is used by Wiccans of all traditions as a protection amulet and to promote spirituality within the home. It is also burned as a traditional herbal incense of the Spring Equinox Sabbat.

AGRIMONY

Witches have used agrimony for protection against evil entities, negativity, sorcery, and poison. In ancient times, it was believed that if a Witch placed this flower under a man's head, he would fall into a deep, sleeplike trance.

AGUE ROOT

The root of the ague plant has been used for centuries as a natural protection amulet against evil and sorcery. It possesses the power to break all hexes, unlucky jinxes, and curses and is used by many modern Witches in uncrossing rituals.

ALTHEA

Althea is used by Witches as both an incense and an herbal amulet for protection against negativity and evil entities. Althea also facilitates the psychic abilities, and it is often used by practitioners of Voodoo magick to attract good spirits.

AMARANTH

Back in the Middle Ages, amaranth was used by necro-mancers to conjure up the spirits of the dead. It was also once believed that a wreath made of amaranth flowers could give a magician the power to control invisibility when worn on the head like a crown.

ANGELICA

The angelica is a mystical plant associated with early Nordic magick and is one of the traditional ritual herbs of the Candlemas and Beltane Sabbats. It was worn as a charm in the fifteenth century to protect against the dreaded plague. (According to folklore, an archangel revealed in a vision that the plant had the power to cure the plague.) In many parts of the world, country peasants believed that angelica possessed the power to guard against evil, and they hung its leaves around their children's necks to protect them against the spells and enchantments of sorcerers. Angelica is both a culinary and a medicinal herb, and according to the seventeenth century herbalist Nicholas Culpepper, it should be gathered when the Moon is in the astrological sign of Leo the Lion.

ANISE

As an herb of the magickal arts, anise leaves are used for protection against wicked supernatural entities and the evil eye. Anise seeds are burned as a meditation incense and used in dream pillows to prevent bad dreams.

ARBUTUS

The arbutus has been used since ancient times by Witches and non-Witches alike for protection against all forces of evil and also to exorcise malevolent ghosts and demonic entities.

ASTER

The aster is a magickal plant used by Witches in all forms of love enchantment and in Sabbat potpourris. It is sacred to all Pagan gods and goddesses and is also one of the traditional ritual herbs of the Autumn Equinox Sabbat.

BALM OF GILEAD

Balm of Gilead has been used by Witches and non-Witches alike for healing and protection against evil. It is valued by magicians for its power to conjure spirits and is a popular herb of love magick (the buds are used in philtres and carried as love-attracting amulets).

BASIL

Basil has been used since ancient times in exorcism and purification rites. It protects against all forms of evil and is said to attract good luck and wealth. This herb (which is also known by the folk name "Witches' herb") is potent in all forms of love enchantment and love divination. In olden times, many Witches were said to have drunk an enchanted flying potion made from basil juice to enable them to fly. Basil is one of the traditional ritual herbs of the Candlemas Sabbat.

BAY

This herb is valued by Witches for its powers to heal, purify, protect, and strengthen. It is used in magickal potions and also burned as an incense to facilitate psychic powers and induce prophetic dream-visions. Bay has been used since ancient times to break hexes, remove family curses, exorcise demons and poltergeists, and guard against lightning. It is also potent as an herb of both love magick and wish magick, and is one of the traditional ritual herbs of the Candlemas and Winter Solstice Sabbats.

BELLADONNA

Also known by the folk name "deadly nightshade," belladonna is an herb of magick that was used mainly in

Witches' flying ointments and magickal poisons. It is a plant associated with sorcery and the goddess Hecate, and its use was popular back in the Middle Ages. Belladonna, which is **extremely poisonous,** is seldom used in the Witchcraft of modern times.

BISTORT

As an herb of Wicca and the magickal arts, bistort is used in spells and as a natural amulet to strengthen psychic powers, promote female fertility, banish evil spirits, and attract wealth. Bistort is often burned with frankincense as a powerful divination incense.

BITTERSWEET

This herb is used by modern Witches of all traditions in spells and magickal sachets for protection against evil, negativity, or illness. Sleeping with bittersweet under your pillow will help erase painful memories of a past love from your mind.

BLACKBERRY

The blackberry (or bramble) is used by Witches in all parts of the world in healing and wealth-attracting spells. It is also considered to be a powerful herb of protection and is used in invocations to the goddess Brigit, an ancient Celtic deity who presides over healing, poetry, sacred wells, and smithcraft (blacksmithing).

BLACK HELLEBORE

In the Middle Ages, it was believed that a Witch or Wizard could attain the power of invisibility by tossing a handful of powdered black hellebore into the air while reciting certain magickal incantations, according to ancient grimoires of magick.

BLADDERWRACK

This herb is used in weatherworking magick, wealth-attracting spells, and magickal sachets to facilitate clairvoyance. It offers protection against accidents or illnesses while traveling by sea and is used in spirit conjurations (especially spirits who dwell within the sea).

BLEEDING HEART

The bleeding heart is potent in all forms of love magick and is used by many modern Witches in the practice of love divination. It is said that this flower is the bringer of bad luck when it is grown indoors; however, a silver coin placed in its pot helps to avert this.

BLOODROOT

The bloodroot is a magickal herb used by Witches as a powerful amulet to attract love. It is also carried or worn to ward off all negative vibrations, protect against evil and harm, and guard against black magick or psychic attack. The roots that are the darkest shade of red are the most magickally potent.

BONESET

This herb is often worn or carried to protect against bad spirits and all things of an evil nature. It possesses the power to drive away poltergeists and demonic entities (such as the succubus and incubus), and is often used by exorcists to "clear" a haunted house. An infusion made from boneset herb and sprinkled around the home will keep unwanted supernatural entities from entering or taking up residence.

BRACKEN

Bracken has been used magickally by Witches in all parts of the world as an herbal protection amulet, in healing spells, and to promote female fertility. Prophetic dreams are induced when bracken is placed underneath your pillow. To make rain fall from the sky, burn a handful of dried bracken in an outdoor fire. This form of weather-working magick was commonly practiced by many Native American medicine men and shamans during times of drought.

BROOM

This is a poisonous plant associated with Witches' broomsticks. "Besom," another name for a Witches broomstick, is also one of the folk names given to this plant. In olden days, broom was used as an ingredient in love philtres and as an herbal amulet to protect against the dark powers of sorcery. The magickal use of this herb also includes exorcism, facilitation of clairvoyant abilities, and purification. Many modern witches who dabble in the ancient art of weatherworking use broom in spells to raise or calm the winds.

BURDOCK

As a magickal herb, burdock has been used in aphrodisiacs, love magick, spells to ward off negativity and protect against evil, and charms to protect against serpents and mad dogs. In the southern regions of the United States, necklaces of burdock were often hung around the necks of babies to cure them of colic.

CATNIP

Catnip is used in all forms of cat magick, healing rituals, love sachets, fertility charms, shapeshifting, and spells to ensure happiness in a home. Catnip is used by some Wiccans and modern Witches to create a psychic bond between them and their cat familiars. This herb can also be used to conjure beneficial spirits and attract good luck.

CINNAMON

Cinnamon has been used by Witches and shamans in healing rituals, aphrodisiacs, and spells to attract money or sexual desire. It stimulates clairvoyant abilities and raises both protective and spiritual vibrations. The oil of the cinnamon plant is used to anoint candles for love goddess invocations, love magick, and spells of passion.

CINQUEFOIL

The five-pointed leaves of the cinquefoil are often carried in mojo bags to increase wealth, good health, love, arcane knowledge, and power. The cinquefoil is also a plant of protection, used for centuries to guard against evil, and break hexes and unlucky jinxes. Divinatory love dreams are induced by sleeping with cinquefoil beneath one's head, according to folklore.

COLTSFOOT

As an herb of Wicca and the magickal arts, coltsfoot leaves have been used in love spells and sachets, smoked in a pipe to produce religious visions, and used as a charm to attain peace and tranquility. In parts of Europe, coltsfoot was used to protect horses against sorcery and illness.

COLUMBINE

Also known as "lion's herb," the columbine is used magickally by both male and female Witches to attract true love or to retrieve a lost lover. This herb has also been successfully used in spells designed to induce courage.

COWSLIP

Also known by the folk name "fairy cup," the cowslip has been used magickally to heal sickness, to guard houses against unwanted intruders, to increase one's physical charm and beauty, and to locate lost objects or buried treasure.

CROCUS

The dried flowers of this magickal plant were used as a vision-invoking incense by the Egyptians of ancient times. The crocus has been used by modern Witches in spells to attract love and promote peace, and as a Spring Equinox altar decoration.

DAISY

As an herb of magick, the daisy has been used by Witches in love magick, love divinations, and spells to attract good luck. To make a lost lover return to you, sleep with a root from a daisy underneath your head. Daisies, which are one of the traditional ritual herbs of the Beltane Sabbat, are also said to be able to magickally make fairies materialize.

DANDELION

The dandelion has been used since early times as a magickal plant of divination, especially where matters of love are concerned. It is used to conjure spirits, facilitate clairvoyant abilities, and make secret wishes come true.

DEADLY NIGHTSHADE—SEE BELLADONNA

DILL

This is an herb of protection. It has been used in various parts of the world since ancient times as an herbal amulet to ward off sorcery, break hexes, and protect against demons and evil ghosts. When hung over the front door, it will keep your home safe from enemies (especially those who envy you). In addition to its powers of protection, the dill is valued by Witches for its magickal ability to attract money and good fortune. Dill is also a potent herb in all forms of love magick and in spells designed to increase desire of a sexual nature.

DRAGON'S BLOOD

The resin from the palm tree *Daemonorops draco* is used by Witches as a magickal incense for various enchantments. Dragon's blood is highly valued as an herb of love magick and protection. It dispels negativity and is good for the exorcism of evil supernatural entities. It is said to restore lost manhood to men who suffer from an impaired sex drive. A magickal ink made from dragon's blood is traditionally used by Witches and magicians for drawing magick word squares and talismans.

ELDER

The elder has been used magickally to break the power of curses, exorcise evil entities, and protect against negative forces and sorcery. Witches and magicians alike have also used the elder in healing rituals and spells to attract good luck, love, and prosperity. The wood of the elder is commonly used to make magick wands. The berries are said to cure insomnia when placed under a pillow. In Bohemia, a spell recited before an elder tree was at one time believed to cure fever. In Italy, elder wood is used to protect a house against thieves as well as to keep serpents at bay. In many parts of England, knots made from elder twigs were carried as charms against rheumatism.

ELECAMPANE

Also known as "elf dock" and "elfwort," the elecampane is an herb of elfin magick. It attracts love and is potent in all amorous enchantments. It offers protection against evil, psychic attack, and demonic possession, according to folklore. When burned as a magickal incense, elecampane strengthens the clairvoyant powers and scrying (divination by gazing) abilities.

FERN

The fern is best known for being an herb of weatherworking magick. When burned, it is said to bring rain. Additionally, it is used for attracting good luck, exorcism of demons and evil spirits, and protection. In the Middle Ages, sorcerers were believed to use fern seeds in spells to master invisibility. As an herbal amulet, ferns are worn or carried in charm bags to protect against toothaches as well as to enable one to locate hidden treasures.

FOXGLOVE

As an herb of the magickal arts, the foxglove is used for communion with underworld deities and to protect against ghosts, evil forces, and sorcery. When grown near the front door of a house, it prevents evil and demons from entering. When grown in a Witch's garden, it will attract fairy-folk.

FRANKINCENSE

The magickal use of frankincense is mainly as an incense which is burned to dispel negativity, purify magickal spaces, protect against evil, aid meditation, induce psychic visions, attract good luck, and honor Pagan deities. Frankincense is very powerful and has been used in Pagan religious rituals and spellcraft since ancient times.

GINSENG

Chinese sorcerers have used the mysterious forked root of the ginseng since ancient times as a love-attracting amulet and as an aphrodisiac. It is potent in all forms of love enchantment and spells that increase sexual potency (especially of men). The root is often used in wish magick, healing rituals, and spells to break the powers of a hex. When burned as a magickal incense, ginseng keeps wicked spirits at bay and offers protection against all forms of evil. Many Witches substitute ginseng for mandrake root when spellcasting. Both roots possess similar magickal properties and are equally as powerful; however, ginseng is easier (and less expensive) to obtain in the United States than a true European mandrake root.

GOLDENROD

As an herb of Wicca and the magickal arts, goldenrod has been used as a divining rod to locate buried treasures. It is also used in love divinations and money spells and carried as a charm to treat rheumatism and to attract good luck to a Witch's house.

HAWTHORN

Also know as "hagthorn," the hawthorn is a tree of protection, magick, and superstition and has long been associated with Witches, fairies, and the craft of Wicca. It is one of the traditional ritual herbs of the Beltane Sabbat and was at one time used throughout Europe as a maypole decoration. The leaves and blossoms of the hawthorn are potent in fertility-increasing spells, fairy magick, and protection spells which guard against lightning, the evil eye, and malevolent supernatural entities.

HAZEL

Divining rods and Witches' wands that are used for drawing circles are often made from the wood of the hazel. This is a highly magickal plant, and all parts of it are used in Wiccan spellcraft. The hazel is said to aid divination, increase fertility, attract good luck, make wishes come true, and protect against fire, lightning, and all evils. In the Middle Ages, many sorcerers wore special crowns made of woven hazel twigs in order to gain the power of invisibility, according to ancient grimoires.

HELLEBORE, HEMLOCK, HENBANE

These three poisonous plants are associated with sorcery and the Black Arts. In the Middle Ages, they were used in Witches' flying ointments and magickal poisons. Black hellebore was used in rituals to exorcise demons and ghosts, and in spells to attain the power of invisibility. It was also used, along with poison hemlock, to induce astral projection. Hemlock was used by many Witches of old in love enchantments and weatherworking magick to produce rain. Modern Witches seldom (if ever) use hellebore, hemlock, or henbane in any magickal spells or rituals because of their extreme toxicity.

HIGH JOHN THE CONQUEROR

This is a popular herb of mojo magick. It is usually carried in a charm bag to attract love and money, break hexes, and protect against evil. High John the Conqueror is also used to make all-purpose anointing oil. Please note: This root is very poisonous and should never be taken internally.

JASMINE

The fragrant flowers of the jasmine have been used by many Witches in love magick and spells which are cast to attract money or induce dreams of a prophetic nature. The jasmine is also one of the traditional ritual herbs of the Spring Equinox Sabbat.

JUNIPER

The juniper is regarded as a powerful herb of protection. It is carried as an amulet and used in spells to guard against accidents, supernatural entities, enemies, disease, and black magick. Since early times, juniper has been used in exorcism rites as well as in love enchantments. It is said to have the power to increase sexual potency in men, and when burned as an incense, it increases psychic powers and breaks curses and the hexes of evil sorcerers.

KAVA-KAVA

In the Pacific islands of Hawaii and Polynesia, the root of the kava-kava plant is highly valued for its magickal potency. It is used in spells to strengthen the psychic powers, induce religious visions, and guard against all evil forces. The kava-kava is said to be a plant of good luck, and its root is often made into a magickal tea.

LADY'S MANTLE

Lady's mantle came to be known as an important magickal plant back in the sixteenth century upon the discovery that overnight dew collected in the funnel-shaped folds of its semiclosed nine-lobed leaves. Alchemically minded scientists of that time regarded dew as a highly magickal substance, and the plant was soon nicknamed Alchemilla, meaning "little magickal one." Lady's mantle is commonly used by modern Witches in sleep sachets and all forms of love magick.

LAVENDER

This fragrant plant is one of the most popular herbs used in the craft of love magick. Its flowers are carried in love-attracting sachets, and its oil is used to anoint candles used in love spells. In addition, lavender is used for healing, purification, the enablement to see spiritual beings, and protection from those who possess the evil eye.

LUCKY HAND ROOT

This mysterious hand-shaped root from an orchid plant is perhaps the most popular (and powerful) root used in

New Orleans hoodoo magick. It brings good luck and money to those who carry it in a mojo bag, guards against hexes and evil, and is often used by out-of-work persons who seek employment. Travelers who wear or carry a lucky hand root are said to be protected from accidents, robberies, and sickness while away from home.

MANDRAKE—SEE CHAPTER 6, "THE MAGICKAL MANDRAKE"

MARIGOLD

This flower is used by Witches as a magickal herb to keep evil entities at bay (especially when spellcasting or performing sacred rituals), inspire prophetic dreams, strengthen psychic powers, attain success in all legal matters, and improve the vision. For protection while sleeping, place marigold flowers under your bed before retiring for the evening. This plant has also been used in divinations to discover the true identity of a thief.

MAY APPLE—SEE CHAPTER 6, "THE MAGICKAL MANDRAKE"

MEADOWSWEET

Also known as "gravel root," "queen of the meadow," and "trumpet weed," the meadowsweet is traditionally gathered on Midsummer. It is potent in all forms of love magick and is used by many modern Witches as an herb of divination to discover the gender of a thief.

MINT

The leaves of the mint plants have been used magickally for healing, attracting money, increasing sexual desire, exorcising evil entities, and protection (especially while traveling). Many practitioners of the magickal arts use mint to conjure beneficial spirits that aid in spellcasting. Mint oil is often used for anointing candles, ritual tools, and healing poppets.

MISTLETOE

The mistletoe has been used magickally and religiously since the days of the ancient Druids. It is traditionally cut with a golden sickle on Midsummer or when the Moon is six days old. Its protective powers are said to be great, and its leaves and berries have been used in various ways to guard against fire, lightning, mischievous fairies, illness, bad luck, nightmares, and all forms of evil. The mistletoe is also an herb of love magick, and at one time it was believed that a magician could make himself invisible by wearing an amuletic necklace made of mistletoe. Locks can magickally be opened with mistletoe (according to folklore), wounds are healed quickly when mistletoe is laid upon them, and conception is aided when it is carried by women desiring to have children. The mistletoe is one of the traditional ritual herbs of the Yuletide season and the Winter Solstice Sabbat.

MOTHERWORT

As an herb of the magickal arts, motherwort has been used in healing rituals, counter-magick, and Chinese immortality spells. This herb has also been used as an all-powerful charm against evil spirits.

MUGWORT

Mugwort is a plant which has been associated with Witchcraft and healing since ancient times. It is known as "Saint John's plant" in the countries of Holland and Germany, and according to folk legend, a girdle made of mugwort was worn by John the Baptist to protect him against harm in the wilderness. In Germany, mugwort girdles were worn to protect the wearer for twelve months against black magick, sickness, evil spirits, and bad luck. In Poitou, they were worn to prevent backache. As an herb of magick, mugwort is also used for breaking hexes cast on animals, counteracting charms, and exorcising spirits of disease. The magickal powers of mugwort are said to be more potent when the plant is gathered on Saint John's Eve. A sachet filled with the herb offers a traveler protection against fatigue, sunstroke, poison, wild beasts, mischievous elves, and unfriendly spirits. Sleeping on a pillow stuffed with mugwort induces psychic dreams and lets a person view his or her entire future. In China, during the time of the Dragon Festival (the fifth day of the fifth Moon), mugwort is hung to keep away evil demons, while in other parts of the world, a crown made from the sprays of the plant is worn as a charm to increase fertility, arouse sexual desire, cure diseases and insanity, and aid in achieving astral projection. Brewed as a tea, often with lemon balm, mugwort is consumed to aid divination, meditation, and psychic development. Mugwort tea is also used by many Witches as a ceremonial potion for Samhain and Full Moon rituals and as a wash to cleanse and consecrate crystal balls, magick mirrors, and quartz crystals.

MULLEIN

Mullein's association with the Craft stretches back to early times. It was believed that Witches used the down on the plant's leaves to make magickal love potions. Mullein guards against black magick and evil supernatural entities and has long been used in the country of India as an exorcism herb. When carried in a mojo bag, it protects against nightmares, negativity, hexes, ill health, demons, cowardice, and attacks by wild animals. Mullein is commonly used as an herb of love divination in the Ozarks region of the United States.

MYRRH

Myrrh is an aromatic gum resin obtained from several trees and shrubs of the genus *Commiphora*, which is native to India, Arabia, and eastern Africa. It is often burned with frankincense as a sacred and magickal incense for purification, consecration, healing, exorcism, and banishing evil. It aids meditative rituals and was burned in ancient Egypt as an offering to the sun god Ra and the goddess Isis. Myrrh oil is used in sabbat potpourris, sachets, and magickal perfumes. It is also used as an anointing oil for altar candles, ritual tools, and magickal paraphernalia. In Christian mythology, myrrh was one of the sacred gifts of the Wise Men from the East to the infant Jesus (Matthew 2:1–12).

OAK

The oak was a sacred tree to the ancient Druid priests, and its leaves, twigs, bark, and acorns have been used in the Wiccan religion and magickal arts for healing, female fertility, male potency, good luck, divination, maintaining health, and attracting money. As an herb of protection, the oak is said to guard against lightning, back luck, and all persons and things that are evil and harmful. According to folklore, carrying an acorn from an oak tree gives immortality to those who are true believers in its powers.

ORCHID

This magickal plant is used in love spells, philtres, and rituals to induce psychic powers. Its root (which is known by the folk names "satyrion root" and "lucky hand") is commonly used in wish magick and New Orleans hoodoo magick to attract good luck and success and for protection against evil, sorcery, and sickness.

PERIWINKLE

As an herb of the magickal arts, periwinkle has been used to cure "devil-sickness" and demonic possession. It has also been used in love spells, money spells, philtres, and charms to obtain grace or protect against bad spirits, wild beasts, serpents, and poison. In medieval Germany, it was a popular magickal ingredient in immortality spells and potions. When wrapped in a houseleek with worms and taken at meals, periwinkle is said to induce love between a man and a woman. In Italy, its flowers are placed on dead children's coffins or graves as wreaths to protect the soul while on its journey to the afterlife. In the country of Wales, this herb is used by necromancers to make spirits materialize in graveyards. In many parts of Europe, it was nicknamed the "sorcerer's violet" because of its strong connection with wizardry and the Craft.

PINE

When gathered on Midsummer's Day, the needles and cones of the pine tree are said to possess strong magickal powers to heal, exorcise evil entities and negative vibrations, increase female fertility, and protect against all harmful persons, things, and situations. Pine needles are often burned to break hexes and return them to the sender, as well as to attract money. Pine oil is used to anoint candles, and the sawdust from the tree's wood is used as an incense base. The pine is one of the traditional ritual herbs of the Winter Solstice Sabbat.

POPPY

The flowers and seeds of the poppy are highly magickal and have been used in spells, potions, and sachets to promote female fertility, attract money, and induce divinatory dreams. The poppy is regarded by many as a plant of good luck, and it is potent in all forms of love enchantment. According to folklore, drinking wine in which poppy seeds have been soaked for two weeks will give a Witch or magician the power to master invisibility.

RAGWORT

This magickal herb was used in medieval times to keep evil spirits and demons at bay. The Greeks used it to protect against charms and sorcery, and in Cornwall, it was commonly believed that Witches used stalks of the plant to ride upon in the dark of night. In Ireland, ragwort was associated with fairy-folk and was given the nickname of "fairies' horse."

ROSE

Nearly all parts of the rose have been used in love spells, enchantments, and transformations. It was (and still is) believed by many to possess aphrodisiac qualities. Rose oil is used in spells to increase courage. Garlands of rosebuds are used by many modern Witches to decorate their Yule tree, while magickal brews made from the buds are said to cause visions of the future to appear in dreams. In British Columbia, roses were sacred to the Thompson Indians and were used ritually to "purify" widows and widowers of the ghosts of their deceased mates. Throughout Germany, it was believed that roses were guarded by dwarfs and fairies, and unless a person asked their permission before picking a rose, he or she would run the risk of losing a hand or a foot. The rose is one of the traditional ritual herbs of the Spring Equinox and Autumn Equinox Sabbats.

ROSEMARY

Since ancient times, rosemary has been used as an herb of protection and exorcism. Also know by the folk name of "elf leaf," it is burned as an incense also to purify, heal, prevent nightmares, preserve youthfulness, dispel depression, attract fairy-folk, and induce sleep. Rosemary is both a culinary herb and an herb of love enchantment. Many Witches have used it in spells designed for provoking lust. Healing poppets are often stuffed with rosemary herb for its powerful curative vibrations.

ROWAN

The rowan tree is one of the most magickal of all trees. It is also known by the folk names of "Witchbane," "Witchen," and "Witchwood," which clearly evidences its centuries-old connection with the Old Religion. All parts of the tree are potent in the arts of spellcraft. Its leaves and berries are used in spells and carried as an herbal amulet to strengthen psychic powers, heal, and protect against lightning strikes, storms, and ghost hauntings. Rowan attracts good luck, power, and success to those who work its natural magick. The wood from the rowan is traditionally used by Witches for making magickal wands and dowsing rods.

RUE

As an herb of the magickal arts, rue is potent in all forms of love enchantment and is rubbed on the body, worn, or carried to ward off sickness and also to speed up recovery from illnesses or operations. Rue has been employed since early times as a hex breaker, a curse lifter, and an herb of exorcism. The ancient Romans praised rue for its ability to protect against the evil eye. Poisons, werewolves, and all negative or evil forces are said to be rendered powerless by the protective magick of rue. This herb is also used to stuff healing poppets and is added to health-restoring incenses.

SAFFRON

The saffron plant has many magickal powers. It is an herb of love enchantment, healing, weatherworking (for raising the wind), and spells and rituals to strengthen the psychic abilities. In ancient times, the Phoenecians used saffron in their fertility rites and in their worship of the Moon and the goddess Ashtoreth. Drinking a potion made from saffron is said to give a woman or man the gift of second sight.

SAGE

Sage is an herb of immortality, protection, and wish magick. When eaten, worn in a horn amulet, or carried in a mojo bag, sage leaves guard against the evil eye. This herb of magick is also reputed to promote wisdom, heal the body, mind, and soul, and attract money. The sage is one of the traditional ritual herbs of the Samhain Sabbat.

SAINT JOHN'S WORT

This is a healing herb associated with magick and the practice of Witchcraft since early times. Saint John's wort, so called because it was traditionally gathered on Saint John's Eve to ward off evil spirits, was hung in doors and windows during the Middle Ages to protect against demonic influences and is a common herb used in exorcisms and antisorcery charms. It is also one of the traditional ritual herbs of the Summer Solstice Sabbat.

SANDALWOOD

Often burned as a magickal incense, the fragrant sandalwood exorcises demons and evil ghosts, conjures beneficial spirits(especially to aid in spellcraft), promotes spiritual awareness, and is said to make wishes come true. Sandalwood is potent in all forms of healing magick and is one of the traditional ritual incenses burned on altars during Lammas Sabbat rites.

SOLOMON'S SEAL

Named after the six-pointed star amulet of mystical power, the Solomon's seal has been used since ancient times as an herb of protection and exorcism. It is often burned as an incense offering to the old gods of the Pagan pantheon. Its root is used to make potions which drive out all demons, negativity, and evil forces when sprinkled.

SUMMER SAVORY

The summer savory is a plant associated with satyrs (mythological half-man/half-goat creatures with insatiable sexual appetites) and was at one time an essential ingredient in love potions and aphrodisiacs. When worn or carried in a mojo bag, this herb is said to strengthen the powers of the mind.

TANSY

As an herb of the magickal arts, tansy has been used in spells for invisibility and immortality and to keep evil ghosts from entering a house. In Sussex, England, tansy leaves were worn in the shoe as a charm against fever. In many parts of Europe, it was worn by women to aid conception and prevent miscarriage. Tansy is one of the traditional ritual herbs of the Spring Equinox Sabbat.

THISTLE

Thistle has been used in healing spells, exorcisms, hex breaking, and spells for protection against thieves, evil, lightning, melancholy, and negative energy. In old England, thistles were used as magickal wands by Wizards. Beneficial spirits can be conjured by boiling thistle in water and gazing into the steam.

THYME

This magickal herb is used in love spells and divinations, dream magick, spells to increase strength and courage, and charms against nightmares. Thyme is also used in healing spells, purifications, and rituals to develop extra-sensory perception.

VALERIAN

As an herb of the magickal arts, valerian is used in all forms of love magick, sleep potions, and purifications. Valerian is also used as an herb of protection. It is said to keep a home safe from lightning strikes, and was used by the ancient Greeks as an amulet to keep away all evil forces and entities.

VANILLA

The vanilla plant is used in love magick. Its beans are used as amulets to improve mental powers, and its purple flowers are used in aphrodisiacs and passion sachets.

VERVAIN

Vervain is a spiky, wayside plant with purplish-blue flowers and a magickal, mystical past. It has been associated with Witches, sorcerers, and magick since the beginning of history. As one of the most magickal herbs of Wicca craft, vervain has been used in wish magick, love potions, aphrodisiacs, divinations, charms, incantations, money-attracting spells, exorcisms, and purifications. Vervain is said to repel evil ghosts and incubi, protect against all forms of sorcery, enchantments, and charms, cure diseases, turn enemies into friends, open locks magickally, protect a home against storms and lightning and enable one to see into the future. Given the appropriate nickname of "enchanter's plant," vervain was used by the ancient Druids in prophecy; the Persians in their worship of the sun; the Romans used it to decorate the altars of Venus and Jupiter; and the Anglo-Saxons carried the plant's root as a charm to cure ulcers. When worn around the neck as a charm, vervain is said to attract good luck and protect the wearer from headaches and the venomous bites of serpents. Many practitioners of ceremonial magick wear a chaplet of vervain for protection when invoking spirits. The plant is traditionally gathered at the time of the Summer Solstice or when the Dog Star is rising.

VETIVERT

Also known as "khus-khus," the vetivert is considered by many to be a very lucky plant. It breaks streaks of bad luck and attracts good luck when worn or carried as a lucky charm. It has been used by Witches in various ways in money-attracting spells, the breaking of hexes, and all forms of love magick. When burned as a magickal incense, vetivert is said to offer protection against thieves and black magick.

VIOLET

The violet has been used in aphrodisiacs, love spells, wish magick, and healing rituals. Violets have also been worn in sachets, herbal amulets, and mojo bags to keep evil spirits at bay, heal wounds, counteract bad luck, and cure insomnia.

WILLOW

The willow symbolizes death and the Underworld. Its leaves, bark, and wood are used in all forms of love magick, healing spells, lunar magick, divination, and spirit conjuring. The willow possesses strong powers of protection and has long been used to avert evil. Willow wood is used for magickal wands, its branches are traditionally used to bind Witches' brooms, and its bark is crushed and burned as an offertory incense to Pagan deities associated with the Moon and its powers.

WITCH HAZEL

The Witch hazel is named for its centuries-old association with Witches and the magickal arts. Its forked branches are used by dowsers as divining rods to locate buried treasure and subterranean water. As an herb of magick, it is used in spells to heal broken hearts and to guard against all evil influences.

WORMWOOD

Also known as "absinthe" and "old woman," the wormwood is carried as an amulet, burned as an incense, and used in magickal potions to strengthen psychic powers, guard against bewitchment, conjure spirits (especially in graveyards or at seances), and counteract poisons. According to folklore, wormwood is effective in keeping sea serpents at bay.

YARROW

As an herb of the magickal arts, yarrow has been worn as a charm against sorcery, demons, negativity, and ghosts; used in love divinations, I Ching divinations, and exorcisms; and hung in houses on Midsummer's Eve to protect the inhabitants against sickness throughout the ensuing year. Many modern Witches have used yarrow in rituals and brews to increase psychic powers, and the herb is often worn at Pagan handfasting ceremonies to dispel negative influences.

Herbal Oils and Their Magickal Properties

Herbal oils are magickally potent and are used by Witches and Wiccans in various ways: They are used in the healing craft of aromatherapy; as sacred anointments for candles, poppets, sachets, and ritual tools; and also for massaging the body. Many are used in the preparation of incenses, perfumes, and potpourris; and the edible ones are often added to Witches' brews, potions, and love philtres.

Essential oils, which are extracted from a plant's petals, leaves, or bark, are believed by many to contain the "soul" or "spirit" of the plant. When used in the proper manner, they can connect a Witch with his or her "inner realms of power."

These oils can be bought in nearly every occult shop or Witchcraft supply catalogue. They are often sold both as individual scents and as blends created for specific magickal or religious purposes.

Acacia: meditation, psychic powers, purification.
Allspice: vitality.
Almond: money.
Apple Blossom: happiness.
Balsam: exorcism, growth, healing, insight, hex breaking, money, and visions.
Basil: harmony.
Bay: female attraction and love magick.
Bayberry: money.
Bergamot: hex breaking and money.
Carnation: power and vitality.
Cedar: courage, hex breaking, and protection.
Clary Sage: happiness, insight, and visions.
Clove: healing, love magick, sexual desire, and purification.
Eucalyptus: healing.
Fir Balsam: money and mystical visions.
Frankincense: hex breaking, prosperity, protection, and purification.
Gardenia: harmony, healing, love magick, male attraction, and peace.
Ginger: healing, love magick, male attraction.

Heliotrope: psychic powers and spirituality.
Honeysuckle: mental powers and money.
Hyacinth: meditation and peace.
Jasmine: love magick, male attraction, meditation, and purification.
Lavender: healing, love magick, male attraction, menopause, purification, sleep, Triple Goddess.
Lemon Balm (Melissa): balance of yin and yang energies.
Lemon Grass: psychic powers.
Lilac: harmony, mental powers, and psychic development.
Lime: healing and sex magick.
Lotus: healing, luck, and spirituality.
Magnolia: meditation, peace, and spirituality.
Mimosa: strengthening of psychic powers.
Mint: money.
Musk: courage, fertility, and male attraction.
Myrrh: female attraction, healing, hex breaking, meditation, protection, purification, sexual desire, and Triple Goddess.
Myrtle: prosperity, protection, and Triple Goddess.
Narcissus: harmony, healing, and sleep.
Nutmeg: happiness, invisibility, marriage, meditation, prosperity, and psychic powers.
Olive: purification.
Orris: love magick.
Patchouli: female attraction, growth, Horned God, love magick, money, and protection against evil, black magick, or psychic attack.
Pine: money.
Rose: love and peace.
Rose Geranium: courage and hex breaking.
Rosemary: healing of body, mind, or spirit, hex breaking, mental powers, power over others, protection, and vitality.
Rue: hex breaking and protection.

Sage: hex breaking, protection, and wisdom.

Sandalwood: growth, healing, love magick, psychic powers, purification, and spirituality.

Sweet Pea: friendship, happiness, and love magick (especially of a platonic nature).

Tonka: male attraction.

Tuberose: happiness, peace, and psychic powers.

Vanilla: power over others, sexual desire, and vitality.

Vervain: fertility and money.

Vetivert: female attraction, hex breaking, love magick, money, and sex-magick.

Violet: female attraction, healing, and protection against bad luck, evil, sorcery or demonic possession.

Wisteria: protection against all forms of evil.

Ylang-Ylang: aphrodisiac, love magick, and sexual desire in both women and men.

3

Herbs of the Enchanted World

Plants Associated With Fairies, Elementals, and Woodland Spirits

If you wish to attract fairy-folk to your yard, plant any of the following herbs in your garden: carnation (especially red ones), clover, cowslip, elder, hollyhock, lilac, lobelia, pansy, primrose (blue and red ones are their favorites), rose, and shamrock.

Earth elementals (also known as "gnomes") are said to be strongly attracted to the foxglove, which has many fairy-inspired nicknames, including fairy fingers, fairy's caps, fairy weed, fairy's thimbles, fairy petticoats, and fairy's glove.

Fire elementals (also known as "salamanders") favor the heliotrope. Air elementals (also known as "sylphs") are drawn to sassafras, and Water elementals (also known as "undines") find all aquatic plants to be irresistible.

To keep your yard and home safe from mischievous fairies or evil-mannered nature spirits of any kind, plant any of the following herbs in your garden or near your house: dill, morning glory, prickly gorse, and rosemary. Fairies cannot stand the sight or smell of these plants, according to folklore.

The peony is another plant reputed to be effective as a natural amulet against evil fairies. To harness its magickal powers, wear a necklace of peony roots carved into small beads and strung together, or put some peony roots or seeds into a consecrated mojo bag and wear it on a string around your neck. You can also carry it in your pocket or purse for protection.

If you hear bluebells ringing in your garden, take care, for it is an omen that an evil fairy or nature spirit is not too far away.

According to European folklore, the fairy race (which is often referred to as the "Good Folks," "Good Neighbours," and "Wee People") like to gather at night around elder trees and in thickets of ash, oak, and hawthorn, which are known in England as "fairy triads." It is there that they dance, sing, frolic, and make magick until the first light of dawn.

Ironically, the same trees that fairies are said to be fond of and even hold sacred are also believed by many superstitious folks around the world to be effective natural amulets to protect against and repel fairy folk as well as other mischievous or malevolent nature spirits.

Other fairy-protection trees are the bay laurel, birch, hazel, and holly.

To keep wicked fairies from riding horses into the night or braiding their manes and tails so that wagoners are unable to brush them, many superstitious horse owners would fasten a tall birch tree dressed with white and red ribbons near the stable door. The tree would remain there for one whole year, and then at Beltane (May 1) it would be taken down and burned, and a new decorated birch tree would take its place.

In Britain it is said that fairies can be seen by the human eye wherever the trees of ash, oak, and hawthorn grow together.

An old wives' tale of unknown origin says that if a mortal man or woman wears the herb of thyme, he or she will have the power to see fairies.

A four-leaf clover upon which seven grains of wheat have been laid will also give a mortal fairy-vision.

At night, when humans are asleep, the "Little People" are said to be busy under the silver rays of the Moon, making magickal fairy brews from dandelions and collecting dew from the tubular flowers of the primrose. It is believed that the dew is the magickal substance which gives them their powers of invisibility.

In the old and enchanted country of Ireland, shamrock (or wood sorrel) is sacred to the leprechauns and will attract them if planted in a secluded garden or woodland. According to an ancient legend, every leprechaun guards a hidden pot of gold, and if any human is lucky enough to catch one, the leprechaun must reveal to that person the location of his treasure. Of course, leprechauns are extremely clever members of the fairy race, and very few, if any, have ever been caught.

A circle of mushrooms growing in a grassy area is called a "fairy ring." This nickname stems from the folk belief that the dancing feet of fairy folk magickally produce the circle. Other explanations for mushroom circles are that they are boundary markers for the magick circles of fairy-witches, and also that they are gateways to the invisible otherworld where the fairies dwell during the daylight hours.

Cattle and sheep are said to avoid fairy rings, and to sleep on one (especially after the sun has gone down) is unwise. Stepping on one will cause the fairies to curse you with bad luck, and picking any of its toadstools is said to cause a death in the family.

Ragwort (*senecio*) is nicknamed "fairies' horse" because at one time it was believed that fairies used their magickal powers to change the plants into fairy-sized horses, which they rode at night. At the crack of dawn, their magick spells would wear off and the fairy horses would change back into ragworts.

Other plants associated with fairies, elves, and woodland spirits are the daisy, elecampane (which is also known as "elfwort" and "elf dock"), and Indian pipe (which is also known as "fairy smoke").

Sacred Herbs of the Voodoo Loas

In the Voodoo religion, the gods and goddesses who take spiritual possession of their devotees are called "loas." Loa is the Congo word for "spirit."

Like the male and female deities of the Pagan pantheon, each Voodoo loa also has a sacred herb dedicated to him or her. The appropriate herb (or a special perfume or incense made from it) is often used in the religious worship, invoking rites, and magickal ceremonies of each loa.

The following list contains the names of the popular Voodoo loas, their descriptions, and the herbs that are sacred to them:

Agwe is a ruler of the sea. He is also the patron loa of all fishermen and sailors, and the consort of Erzulie, the loa of love and beauty. The herb sacred to Agwe is the lavender.

Aizan is a Haitian god who dwells within water. It is said that when he possesses his devotees, he gives them the power to heal and to divine the future. The herb sacred to Aizan is angelica.

Ayida Wedo is a Haitian and Dahomean loa who manifests in the form of a rainbow-serpent of many colors. She is the consort of the serpent loa Damballah and is often symbolized by a snake, serpent, or dragon. The herb sacred to Ayida Wedo is the hyacinth.

Baron Samedi is a loa who presides over both death and black magick. Envisaged as a dwarf with a black coat and top hat, he is the ruler of cemeteries who controls the souls of those whose lives have been taken by evil magick. The herb sacred to Baron Samedi is myrrh.

Bosu is a Haitian god whose sacred color is black. He inhabits mountains and cemeteries, and the herb sacred to him is the apple blossom.

Carrefour is an ancient Voodoo loa known as the Master of the Crossroads and identified with the loa called Papa Legba. He is worshipped mainly by practitioners of black magick who belong to the Petro cult. The herb sacred to Carrefour is frankincense.

Damballah is a Voodoo loa known as the Serpent of the

Sky, the Father of the Falling Waters, and loa of all spiritual wisdom. He is the consort of Ayida Wedo, the rainbow-serpent loa, and is worshipped and invoked on Thursdays. The herb sacred to Damballah is the lilac blossom.

Erzulie is the Voodoo loa of love, beauty, and femininity. She is the consort of both Ogoun and Agwe, and is worshipped and invoked on Fridays. The herb sacred to Erzulie is the rose.

Ghede is a loa who presides over both death and healing. He is worshipped and invoked on Saturdays and at the close of every ceremony. He is said to manifest in the form of a clown or court jester wearing a giant wooden phallus between his legs. The herb sacred to Ghede is myrrh.

Legba (who is also known as Papa Legba) is the Voodoo loa of pathways and crossroads and was at one time a Dahomean sun god. He appears in the form of an old peasant man with a limp and is considered to be the most important loa of the Voodoo pantheon. He is the guardian and keeper of the keys that unlock the gate separating the material world from the world of spirit. Every Voodoo ceremony begins with a special invocation to him. The herb sacred to Papa Legba is frankincense.

Loco (also known as Papa Loko Dahomey) is a Haitian Voodoo loa of healing. He is also said to be the spirit of herbs and vegetation who gives healing power to leaves. His sacred color is green, and the herb sacred to him is the pine.

Ogoun is a Haitian and Nigerian loa who presides over fire and battle. He protects his worshippers from bullets or wounds inflicted by weapons, and is invoked with the ceremonial pouring of rum which is then set on fire.

Ogoun is worshipped and invoked on Wednesdays, his symbol is the sword, and the herb sacred to him is the cinnamon tree.

Simbi is a loa known as the Patron of Magickal Powders. He is invisible and lives inside mango and calabash trees. He is worshipped and invoked on Tuesdays, and the herb sacred to him is patchouli.

Sobo is a Haitian and Dahomean loa of thunder and lightning, whose sacred symbol is the ram. According to Voodoo belief, Sobo forges sacred thunderstones by hurling to the earth a thunderbolt that strikes a rock outcropping and casts a stone to the floor of the valley. Before a houngan (a Voodoo priest) may touch it with his hands, the thunderstone must lie there for a year and one day. The herb sacred to Sobo is Saint John's wort.

Ti Kita is a powerful female loa associated with the cult of magick and the dead. Pigs and goats are ritually sacrificed to appease her. Her magickal color is black, and the herb sacred to her is the orange blossom.

Zaka is a Haitian loa who presides over all forms of agriculture. It is said that he manifests in the form of a peasant man wearing a straw hat, smoking a pipe, and carrying a machete in his hand. The herb sacred to Zaka is the honeysuckle.

Herbs of Mythology

Trees and flowers play a major role in most ancient myths, especially those of Greek and Roman origin. They are sacred to the gods and goddesses, as well as to the heroes, enchantresses, and nymphs. They possess the powers of magick, healing, prophecy, protection, and transformation. Some are good, some are evil, and some are actually divine beings, nymphs, or mortals who have been changed into plant form by the will of the gods or by magickal spell.

The magick of herbs is an important part of nearly every ancient and contemporary religion (Christian, non-Christian, and pre-Christian alike) and there probably isn't one tree or flower which hasn't at one time, somewhere in the world, been sacred to a particular deity or associated with a myth, fable, or folktale.

Even the Bible contains tales of plant oracles (the burning bush which spoke to Moses); mandrake aphrodisiacs (mentioned in both the Song of Solomon and the Book of Genesis); magickal rods of poplar, almond, and plane trees; and trees bearing fruits of temptation, just to name a few.

The botanical names of many plants come from the names of ancient Pagan goddesses and mythological creatures. For instance, the genus *Artemesia* is named after Artemis, the virgin goddess of the hunt and the Moon. The genus *Euonymus* is named after Euonyme, an ancient Greek deity known as the "Mother of the Furies". The botanical name for eyebright (*Euphrasia officinalis*) is derived from Euphrosyne, the name of one of the three Graces. Her name means "mirth," and like her two other sisters, she dispensed charm and beauty and presided over the dance, the banquet, and all social enjoyments and arts of elegance. *Satureja* (savory) is a derivative of the Latin word for "satyr" (a woodland god in the form of a man from the waist up and a goat from the waist down). *Centaurium* (centaury) and *Centaurea* (cornflower, knapweed) get their names from the wise centaur Chiron, who was renowned for his skill in the art of medicine as well as in the arts of hunting, music, and prophecy.

Myrrh (*Commiphora myrrha*) takes its name from a princess named Myrrha, who (by the power of Aphrodite) was made to fall in love with her father, King Cinyras. When the aging king discovered that his secret lover was actually his own daughter in disguise, he ordered her to pay for her insatiable desires with her life. The gods of Mount Olympus intervened and transformed Myrrha into a myrtle tree, the resin of which produces the fragrance myrrh. Ten months later, as a result of the incestuous affair between daughter and father, the tree gave birth to the handsome god Adonis, who was delivered with the tusk of a wild boar.

The blood-red anemone (or windflower) is sacred to Adonis, who met his death after being gored by a mad boar. An ancient legend says that in each place where his divine blood had stained the Earth, his crimson flower sprung up.

In ancient Greece, young women mourned for him during his annual rite, and rejoiced for him each season when the anemone bloomed.

A similar legend claims that a plant known as the pheasant's eye was the flower that sprung up from the blood of Adonis. The botanical name of this plant, *Adonis annua*, is dedicated to this handsome young god who was cherished by Aphrodite, the beautiful goddess of love.

The mint (*Mentha*) takes its name from the beautiful nymph named Minthe, who was unfortunately turned into an aromatic mint plant by the jealous goddess Persephone after Persephone learned that her beloved Pluto was smitten with love for the fair nymph.

Narcissus was a handsome youth who was a scorner of love. One day the goddess Nemesis cast a spell over him to make him fall in love with his own reflection in a pool of clear water. He pined away, gazing at his own reflection and burning with love for his own self. After he died and his soul was taken to the Underworld, his body transformed into a flower which was given his name—the narcissus.

Yarrow was said to have been used by the Greek hero Achilles during the Trojan War to heal the battle wounds of his soldiers. The botanical name of the yarrow (*Achillea millefolium*) reflects this myth.

According to legend, the elecampane grew from the tears that had been shed by Helen of Troy. The plant's botanical name (*Inula helenium*) is derived from her name.

The bay laurel tree, whose Latin name (*Laurus nobilis*) translates to "renowned bay tree," was declared a sacred tree by the sun god Apollo after his beloved nymph Daphne was magickally transformed into one by her father, Peneus. In remembrance of and dedication to Daphne, Apollo wore a wreath of laurel leaves upon his head at all times.

Paralisos, the son of Flora and Priapus, was magickally and permanently transformed into a cowslip after he died of a broken heart over the loss of his beloved.

The poplar tree was the type of tree which the grief-stricken Heliades changed themselves into after seeing their brother fall from the sky. A crown of poplar leaves was worn by Hercules when he ventured into the dark and dangerous realm of the Underworld to retrieve Cerberus, the monstrous three-headed dog who guarded the gates of Hades.

Tansy, which takes its name from the Greek word *athanasia* (meaning "immortality"), was the main ingredient in a magickal potion which made the Trojan boy Ganymede immortal. He was then carried away by Zeus to be the eternal cupbearer to the gods.

Parsley was the plant chosen by Hercules for his garlands; and according to ancient Greek legend, in the spot where the blood of the fallen hero Archemorus ("forerunner of death") was spilled, parsley sprang up.

Violets sprang up where Orpheus slept, and roses sprang up from the blood of Aphrodite, who stepped on a thorn while trying to help Adonis.

To the Turks, the red rose is from the blood of the prophet Muhammad.

Garlic, which has been used since ancient times to protect against evil, black magick, vampires, and other malevolent supernatural creatures, was believed to have been the herb called "moly" which was given to Ulysses by Mercury to prevent the sorceress Circe from magickally transforming him into a swine.

According to an ancient Islamic legend, when Satan was banished from the Garden of Eden, garlic sprang up from the ground where his left foot touched, and onions sprang up from the ground where his right foot touched.

The aconite was said to have grown wild on a hill in ancient Greece known as Aconitus. On this flower-covered hill, Hercules battled the hellhound Cerberus. When the foam from the creature's mouth touched the aconites, their violet-blue hooded flowers turned poisonous and deadly.

Aconite was the poison used by the goddess Hecate to kill her father, and by the sorceress Medea to kill Theseus, the minotaur-slaying hero of Attica.

The poisonous berries of the deadly nightshade (*Atropa belladonna*) were used by Atropos (one of the three fates) to sever the thread of life.

Mistletoe, the most sacred and magickal of all plants to the ancient Druid priests, is associated with the thunder god Thor in the country of Sweden.

According to Germanic mythology, the god Balder was accidentally killed by a spear of mistletoe thrown by his blind brother Hodur.

In Virgil's *Aeneid*, the hero Aeneus was protected by a golden bough of mistletoe which he picked before journeying through the dark and dangerous Underworld.

According to Teutonic mythology, the flowering herb known as flax (or linseed) was under the divine protection of Hulda, the gift-bearing goddess of ploughs, crops, spinning, and weaving. The growing of flax and the spinning of its stalk fibers into linen was an art taught to humans by Hulda herself.

The narcissus, a plant which the ancient Greeks associated with death and the Underworld, enticed the goddess Persephone with its beauty. When she reached out to pick the flower, a chasm opened in the ground before her, and Hades emerged. He was instantly taken with Persephone's youthfulness and beauty and abducted her. Against her will, she was carried down to the Underworld and made to be his wife. Zeus ordered Persephone's release, but because she had eaten a forbidden pomegranate seed, she was committed to be Hades' consort for all eternity and could only leave the Underworld for two-thirds of the year (Spring and Summer). When she returns each year to the realm of Hades, her mother, the goddess Demeter, mourns and changes the season to winter.

The mulberry tree is associated with the sad tale of Pyramus and Thisbe, two young Babylonian lovers who took their lives by the sword under a white mulberry tree. Their blood seeped into the ground and touched the tree's roots, causing its white berries to turn red. The gods, saddened by the lovers' suicide, forever changed all white mulberry fruit to red as a memorial to the spilled blood of Pyramus and Thisbe.

All oak trees are sacred to Zeus, the principal deity of the ancient Greek religion and one of the twelve great gods of Mount Olympus. They represent his enduring strength and were used by oracular priests at a sacred oak grove at Dodona to declare the god's divine will.

Another sacred tree was the ash. It was the favorite tree of Ares (the Greek god of war and the son of Zeus), and in Norse mythology, a giant ash tree called Yggdrasil was believed to have united Earth, Heaven, and the Underworld by its roots and branches.

The roots of the fig (a tree revered by the ancient

Romans) saved the lives of the wolf-raised twin brothers, Romulus and Remus, by entangling them as they drifted down the Tiber River.

Sacred Trees and Flowers

Nearly all gods and goddesses of ancient Greek and Roman mythology (as well as the deities of other Pagan pantheons such as the Phoenician, Babylonian, Egyptian, etc.) have one or more favorite trees or flowers which are either sacred to them or associated with them.

The following is a list of Pagan deities, nymphs, and heroes (arranged alphabetically), followed by their sacred trees and flowers:

Terra cotta vase, circa 600 B.C., depicting scenes from Greek mythology. (Archaeological Museum, Florence, Italy)

The Greek Pantheon

Adonis (the personification of male beauty): anemone (red), bay laurel, false hellebore, fennel, lettuce, myrrh, and rose.

Aphrodite (goddess of love and passion): anemone, apple, benzoin, campion, cinnamon, crocus, cypress, daisy, mandrake, marjoram, myrrh, myrtle, orris root, palm, parsley, periwinkle, quince, rose, and violet.

Apollo (god of the sun, fertility, prophecy and oracles, and also a deity associated with light, healing, music, and poetry): anise, apple, bay laurel, cypress, date palm, dogwood, fenugreek, heliotrope, hyacinth, jimsonweed, lily of the valley, mistletoe, olive, sunflower, and tamarisk.

Ares (god of battle, identified with the Roman war god Mars): ash and oak.

Artemis (goddess of the Moon, hunting, and wild beasts; equivalent to the Roman Moon goddess Diana): almond, amaranth, artemesia, bay laurel, cedar, cypress, daisy, date palm, fir, hazel, hyacinth, moonwort, mugwort, myrtle, sagebrush, Saint John's wort, tarragon, willow, and wormwood.

Athena (goddess of wisdom and the arts): apple, fir, and olive.

Atropos (one of the three Fates): belladonna.

Chiron (fabled centaur and mentor to many Greek heroes, including Achilles, Jason, and Hercules): centaury, cornflower, and yarrow.

Chloris (goddess of flowers): all beautiful flowers, but especially the rose.

Circe (enchantress who used magickal potions to turn men into swine): belladonna, mandrake, and mullein.

Demeter (corn goddess, mother of Persephone, and personification of the fruitful Earth): bean, corn poppy, myrrh, oak, pennyroyal, poppy, rose, sunflower, vervain, and wheat.

Dionysus (god of wine, ecstasy, nature, and fertility who was worshipped in frenzied orgies): agaric, apple, beech, fennel, fig, fir, grape, ivy, myrtle, pimpernel, pine, and walnut.

Dryads (tree-dwelling nymphs): elder and oak.

Eos (winged goddess of dawn): saffron.

Eros (god of love and sexual desire): bay laurel and rose.

The Fates (three goddesses who presided over the course of human life): cypress.

Gaia or Gaea (Mother Earth): aspen and bay laurel.

Ganymede (handsome Trojan youth who became the eternal cupbearer and lover of the god Zeus): coconut, mistletoe, olive, and tansy.

Hades (god of the underworld and ruler of the dead): cypress, narcissus, and oak.

Hebe (goddess of eternal youth): cypress.

Hecate (goddess of the Moon and protectress of all Witches): aconite, almond, azalea, belladonna, cyclamen, dandelion, date palm, garlic, hemlock, lavender, mandrake, mints, monkshood, myrrh, oak, osiers, willow, wolfsbane, and yew.

Helios (god of the sun): bay laurel and heliotrope.

Hera (wife of Zeus and goddess of marriage and childbirth): apple, iris, lily, oak, orris root, pomegranate, and willow.

Hermes (god of commerce and invention, and a messenger and herald for the other gods): almond, lotus, palm, purslane, verbena, vervain, and willow.

Hestia (goddess of the hearth; similar to the Roman goddess Vesta): lavender.

Hyacinthus (god of springtime flowers and lover of the god Apollo): hyacinth.

Hymen (god of marriage and wedding feasts): hawthorn.

Hypnos (god of sleep): opium poppy.

Io (deified priestess of Hera): violet.

Iris (goddess of the rainbow and a messenger of the gods): iris, orris root, and wormwood.

Medea (evil sorceress and daughter of King Phineus): aconite.

Menthe or Mintha (nymph who was transformed into a

mint plant by the jealous goddess Persephone): mints.

Myrrha (daughter and lover of King Cinyras): myrrh.

Nyx (goddess of night and darkness): all night-blooming flowers.

Orpheus (god of the lyre): violets and willow.

Pan (horned god of woodlands, fields, shepherds, and fertility): blessed thistle, fir, oak, pimpernel, pine, and reeds.

Persephone (queen of the underworld): dittany of Crete, narcissus, parsley, pomegranate, poplar, poppy, vervain, and willow.

Phaeton (son of Helios): poplar.

Poseidon (lord of the sea): ash, olive, and pine.

Prometheus (a Titan who fashioned the first man out of clay): fennel.

Rhea (Earth goddess): myrrh, oak, and pine.

Satyrs (anthropomorphic woodland deities): savory.

Selene (lunar goddess): moonwort and rowan tree.

Uranus (Father Sky, the consort of Gaea): ash tree and pomegranate.

Zeus (ruler of Heaven and Earth, and a master of thunderbolts and shapeshifting; the most powerful of the ancient Greek gods): almond, apple, aspen, banyan tree, daisy, fig, mistletoe, oak, olive, orange, peppermint, poplar, sage, and violet.

The Roman Pantheon

Aesculapius (god of healing): bay laurel, lily of the valley, and peach.

Aradia (daughter of the goddess Diana and "founder of the Witch cult on Earth"): rue and vervain.

Aurora (goddess of dawn): rose and saffron.

Bacchus (god of wine and gaiety; similar to the Greek wine-god Dionysus): beech, fig, fir, grape, ivy, and orchid.

Ceres (goddess of fertility and marriage): bay laurel, chaste tree, oak, pomegranate, poppy, rye, wheat, and willow.

Consus (god of stored harvest, good counsel, secret deliberations, and the Underworld): dogwood.

Cupid (winged cherub-god of love, son of the goddess Venus): cypress and rose.

Diana (lunar goddess who also presided over hunting, similar to the Greek goddess Artemis): acacia, apple, beech, dittany of Crete, fir, hazel, jasmine, mandrake, moonwort, mugwort, mulberry, oak, poppy, rue, verbena, vervain, and wormwood.

Euphrosyne (one of the three Graces): eyebright.

Faunus (god of nature, woodlands, and fertility): bay laurel and ilex.

Flora (goddess of flowers): cornflower, rose, and all fruit-bearing trees, especially apple, avocado, cherry, fig, hawthorn, mulberry, olive, peach, pear, and plum.

Hercules (deified hero distinguished for his superhuman strength): all-heal, apple, beech, cypress, parsley, and poplar.

Janus (double-faced god of gates, doorways, journeys, and the beginnings of things): oak.

Juno (protectress of all women, especially those in childbirth; originally a goddess of the Moon): fig, iris, lily, lotus, myrrh, and vervain.

Jupiter (god of wisdom, thunder and lightning): almond, carnation, cypress, gorse, houseleek, mistletoe, mullein, oak, olive, and vervain.

Mars (god of battle): ash, bay laurel, dogwood, fig, garlic, oak, rue, and vervain.

Mercury (messenger of the gods): almond, anise, hazel, palm, pomegranate, storax, willow, and vervain.

Minerva (goddess of arts and handicrafts): mulberry bush, olive, and thistle.

Neptune (god of the sea): ash.

Ops (goddess of fertility and consort of Saturn): all herbs associated with fertility.

Paralisos (son of Flora and Priapus): cowslip and primrose.

Pluto (god of the dead and ruler of the underworld): cypress, fig, mints, oak, and poplar.

Pomona (goddess of fruits and fertility): all fruit-bearing trees, especially apple, avocado, cherry, fig, mulberry, olive, peach, pear, and plum.

Saturn (god of the harvest): cypress, lavender, mandrake, myrrh, pomegranate, and yew.

Sylvanus (god of forests, fields, and herding; depicted as a bearded satyr): pimpernel and pine.

Venus (goddess of love and beauty): anemone, angelica, apple, apricot, aster, benzoin, campion, cinnamon, crocus, daisy, elder, lily, linden, maidenhair fern, marjoram, mistletoe, myrtle, parsley, pimpernel, plantain, quince, raspberry, rose, sandalwood, strawberry, vervain, and violet.

The Egyptian Pantheon

Illustration from an ancient Egyptian papyrus containing the *Book of the Dead*.

Aah (one of the sacred Moon gods of ancient Egypt): moonwort and all herbs under the astrological influence of the Moon.

Amen-Ra (supreme deity of Thebes, king of the gods, and a ruler of life, reproduction, and agriculture): olive.

Bast (cat-headed goddess of fertility, daughter of Isis): catnip and sycamore.

Hathor (celestial cow and sacred star-mother): grape, mandrake, myrtle, rose, and sycamore.

Horus (falcon-headed god of the sky, son of Isis and Osiris): horehound, iris, lotus, oak, and sycamore.

Isis (mother goddess of fertility, magick, and enchantment): date palm, fig, heather, iris, lotus, myrrh, onion, orris root, rose, sycamore, and vervain.

Khons (one of the sacred Moon gods of ancient Egypt): all plants ruled by the Moon.

Min (fertility god): all herbs associated with fertility.

Mut (fertility goddess): all herbs associated with fertility and reproduction.

Nepthys (sister of the goddess Isis): lily.

Osiris (god of vegetation and fertility; brother and consort of the goddess Isis): acacia, dittany of Crete, ivy, lotus, orris root, sycamore, and willow.

Ra (god of the sun): acacia, bay laurel, frankincense, heliotrope, myrrh, olive, and sycamore.

Sekhmet (lion goddess of battle): catnip.

Set or Seth (god of dark powers and brother/murderer of Osiris): all herbs and trees associated with sorcery and the left-hand path.

Thoth (god of the moon, wisdom, magick, arts and science): almond, birch, moonwort, nettle, and storax.

The Celtic Pantheon

Angus (god of love and all things beautiful): rose and all golden-colored flowers.

Anu (mother goddess and a deity who presided over death and the dead): tamarisk.

Brigit, Brigid, or Bride (goddess of fire, wisdom, poetry, and sacred wells; also a deity associated with divination, prophecy, and healing): blackberry and dandelion.

Cernunnos (horned nature god of wild animals, hunting, and fertility): all herbs and trees associated with fertility.

Cerridwen or Kerridwen (Druidic lunar goddess who brewed a sacred cauldron of inspiration with herbs of magick): vervain.

Daghda or Dagda (principal god of the Pagan tribes of Ireland and also a fertility deity): oak.

Epona (mare goddess): coltsfoot.

Lugh (ancient sun god): corn and grain.

Olwen (Welsh/Celtic goddess of love): apple tree and trefoil.

Rhiannon (Welsh/Celtic mother goddess): coltsfoot.

Tara (redeemer goddess): oak.

The Norse Pantheon

Balder or Baldur (god of light): elecampane, oak, oxeye daisy, and Saint John's wort.

Frey (god of fertility and brother of Freya): apple.

Freya (goddess of love, beauty, and the art of healing): cowslip, daisy, elderberry, flax, mistletoe, primrose, rose, and strawberry.

Frigga (mother goddess, consort of Odin, and patroness of marriage and fecundity): mistletoe and strawberry.

Idunn (goddess of spring who possessed the golden apples of eternal youth): wild Scandinavian apple.

Loki (god of fire and mischief; known as both "the Wizard of Lies" and "the Trickster"): storax.

Njord (god of the sea): all oceanic plants.

Odin (god of wisdom, magick, art, and poetry): ash, barley, elecampane, elm, mistletoe, and oak.

Thor (sky god, master of thunderbolts, son of Odin): ash tree, birch, daisy, gorse, hazel, houseleek, oak, rowan

tree, thistle, tormentil, and vervain.
Vor (goddess of marriage): Solomon's seal.

The Persian Pantheon

Ahura Mazda (the creator god): cypress.
Anaitis (goddess of fertility): all flowers and trees associated with fertility.
Mithras (god of light, truth, and justice): cypress.
Ohrmazd or Ormazd (god of light): cypress.
Sol (god of the sun): heliotrope and sunflower.
Zurvan (god of time): century plant.

The Babylonian Pantheon

Ea (god of water, lord of wisdom, and patron of magick and all arts and crafts): cedar.
Ishtar (goddess of love and fertility who was also a queen of battle): acacia and wheat.
Lilith (a demon-goddess who carried souls down into the Underworld): lily and tarragon.
Mylitta (a goddess identified with both Ishtar and Aphrodite): all flowers and trees associated with fertility.
Shamash (god of the sun and brother of the goddess Ishtar): all herbs associated with prophecy.
Sin (god of the Moon; identified with the Sumerian god Nanna): moonwort and all white flowers.

Brahma, the all-seeing god. (Victoria and Albert Museum, London, England.)

The Hindu Pantheon

Brahma (first aspect of the Trimurti, or Hindu Trinity): fig, lotus, oak, olive, and poplar.

Cunti (goddess of fecundity): ginseng and lotus.

Ganesh (elephant-headed god of wisdom, prudence, and learning): sesame.

Hanuman (sacred monkey god worshipped by wrestlers and women who desired children): palm.

Indra (warrior god): olive.

Kali (ferocious goddess of death and consort of Shiva): cannabis.

Kama (handsome god of love and the personification of desire): sugar cane.

Karttikeya (six-faced god of battle): all flowers and trees bearing thorns.

Krishna (the most beloved of all the Hindu deities): basil.

Lakshmi (goddess of the lotus, wealth, and good fortune; also a goddess who presides over the act of lovemaking): basil and lotus blossoms.

Maya or Queen Maya (mother of Buddha): cherry tree.

Parvati (goddess of mountains and consort of Shiva): all flowers and trees associated with the Moon and lunar magick.

Sarasvati (goddess of wisdom and eloquence; originally a river goddess worshipped for her purifying and fertilizing powers): palm tree.

Shiva (one of the three supreme gods of the Hindu Trinity): banyan tree and marjoram.

Surya (god of the sun): water lily.

Vishnu (one of the three supreme gods of the Hindu Trinity): basil, banyan tree, bodhi tree, jasmine, and marjoram.

Yama (judge of the dead): sesame.

The Aztec Pantheon

Centeotl (god of corn): the maize plant.

Quetzalcoatl (feathered serpent god of fertility, wind, and wisdom): maize plant, snakeroot, windflower.

Tlazolteotl (the "mother of all gods" who presided over love): all Venus-ruled plants and those associated with lovers and the Pagan art of love magick.

Xilonen (maize goddess): maize plant.

Xochipilli (god of love): all flowers are sacred to him.

Xochiquetzal (goddess of love and flowers; Moon virgin and fairy queen): marigold and all flowers associated with fertility.

Xolotl (patron god of magicians): all flowers and trees under the astrological influence of the planet Venus.

Gods and Goddesses From Around the World

Arrianrhod (Welsh mother goddess): all flowers and trees associated with fertility.

Ashtoreth (Phoenician goddess of the Moon): cypress, myrtle, and saffron.

Astarte (Phoenician goddess of love and fertility): acacia, cypress, lily, myrtle, palm, and pimpernel.

Attis (Phrygian god of fertility and vegetation, consort of the fertility goddess Cybele): almond, ivy, pimpernel, pine, and violet.

Baal (Phoenician god of nature and fertility, associated with winter rain): frankincense and palm.

Bau (Sumerian fertility god): all flowers and trees associated with fertility.

Belili (Sumerian goddess of love, the ruler of the Underworld, and an ancient deity who ruled over trees, wells, and springs): willow.

Buddha (Chinese god): acacia, bay laurel, bodhi (or bo-tree), lotus, and plumeria.

Cybele (Phrygian goddess of nature and fertility): fir, myrrh, oak, pimpernel, pine.

Elle Woman (Danish spirit-goddess of the elder tree): all elder trees.

Eostre (Saxon goddess of fertility and springtime whom the holiday of Easter was originally named after): cinquefoil, crocus, daffodil, Easter lily, iris, and rose.

Inanna (Sumerian mother goddess and a deity who presided over both love and war; identified with the Babylonian goddess Ishtar): reeds.

Kuan Yin (Chinese goddess of healing and mercy): lily.

Kubaba (a goddess of love and an ancient mother-goddess worshipped throughout Asia Minor): pomegranate.

Kupala (Slavic goddess of life, lovemaking, and vitality): birch, loosestrife, maidenhair fern, and saxifrage.

Laka (Polynesian rainstorm goddess and patroness of all hula dancers): ferns.

Maui (Polynesian god of war, a trickster-god and culture hero who was believed to have created the lands of the Earth): banyan tree.

Mescalito (Mexican spirit-deity of the peyote cactus; said to appear in visions to those who ritually use peyote): peyote.

Nu Kua (Chinese goddess known as "the Creatress"): reeds.

Ostara (German fertility goddess, identified with the Saxon goddess Eostre): lily.

Pattini (Singhalese goddess of marriage): mango tree.

Pele (Hawaiian fire goddess who is said to live in the crater of the Kilauea volcano): ti plant (also known as "good luck plant").

Poppy Goddess (a benevolent Minoan goddess worshipped by the women of ancient Crete): opium poppy.

Shadrafa (a Phoenician god of healing and the conqueror of evil): all healing herbs.

Shakti (Tibetan counterpart of the Egyptian war goddess Sekhmet, and a deity associated with eternal life): gotu kola.

Tane (Polynesian sky god and lord of fertility): all flowers associated with fertility.

Thunor (ancient Germanic god of thunder and lightning): all flowers and trees associated with fertility.

Woden (ancient Germanic god of war, skald-craft [poetry], prophecy and the arts of magick): ash tree.

4

Sabbat Herbs

Candlemas

The Candlemas Sabbat is celebrated by Wiccans on the second day of February. It is one of the four Major (or Great) Sabbats celebrated each year, and is also known as Imbolc, Imbolg, Lady Day, and Oimelc.

The traditional ritual herbs of the Candlemas Sabbat are angelica, basil, bay, benzoin, celandine, heather, myrrh, and all yellow flowers.

77

The traditional herbal incenses burned on this Sabbat are basil, myrrh, and wisteria.

Some Wiccans decorate their altars with a sprig of evergreen or a homemade besom made of dried broom to symbolize the "sweeping out of the old."

Spring Equinox

Celebrated by Wiccans on the first day of Spring, the Spring Equinox Sabbat is one of the four Minor (or Lesser) Sabbats celebrated each year and is also known as the Vernal Equinox Sabbat, Festival of the Trees, Alban Eilir, Ostara, and Rite of Eostre.

The traditional ritual herbs of the Spring Equinox Sabbat are acorns, celandine, cinquefoil, crocus, daffodil, dogwood, Easter lily, honeysuckle, iris, jasmine, rose, strawberry, tansy, and violets.

The traditional herbal incenses burned on this Sabbat are African violet, jasmine, rose, sage, and strawberry.

Springtime wildflowers (in baskets, vases, or just by themselves) make beautiful herbal decorations for Sabbat altars and circles. If your coven celebrates the Spring Equinox with a crowning-of-the-Spring-Queen ritual, use yellow flowers such as daffodils, forsythia, gorse, and primrose for her bouquet and chaplet.

Beltane

The Beltane Sabbat is celebrated by Wiccans on May Eve (the last day of April), in the evening, and the first day of May. It is one of the four Major (or Great) Sabbats celebrated each year and is also known as May Day, Cyntefyn, Rood Day, Rudemas, and Walpurgisnacht.

The traditional ritual herbs of the Beltane Sabbat are almond, angelica, ash tree, bluebells, cinquefoil, daisy, frankincense, hawthorn, ivy, lilac, marigold, mead-owsweet, primrose, roses, satyrion root, woodruff, and yellow cowslips.

The traditional herbal incenses burned on this Sabbat are frankincense, lilac, and rose.

A daisy chain and springtime wildflowers are herbal decorations used by many Wiccans for their Beltane altars and circles (in addition to the traditional maypole, which symbolizes fertility and the sacred union of male and female). Blackthorn and hawthorn are the traditional trees of this Sabbat, and in some covens, it is a Beltane custom for the female members to wear chaplets made from their blossoms (with thorns removed, of course). In these covens, the High Priest usually wears a chaplet made of oak leaves to symbolize the Oak King.

Summer Solstice

The Summer Solstice Sabbat is celebrated by Wiccans on the first day of Summer. It is one of the four Minor (or Lesser) Sabbats celebrated each year and is also known as Midsummer, Litha, and Alban Hefin.

The traditional ritual herbs of the Summer Solstice Sabbat are chamomile, cinquefoil, elder, fennel, hemp, larkspur, lavender, male fern, mugwort, pine, roses, Saint John's wort, wild thyme, wisteria, and verbena.

The traditional herbal incenses burned on this Sabbat are frankincense, lemon, myrrh, pine, rose, and wisteria.

The altar decorations for this Sabbat usually consist mainly of summertime flowers. It is a custom among some covens to place heather on the Sabbat altar, which is sprinkled with water by the High Priestess as part of the Midsummer ritual. Aromatic and bright-colored flowers of the season are used to make the High Priestess's chaplet.

Lammas

The Lammas Sabbat is celebrated by Wiccans on the first day of August. It is one of the four Major (or Great) Sabbats celebrated each year and is also known as Lughnasadh, August Eve, and the First Festival of Harvest.

The traditional ritual herbs of the Lammas Sabbat are acacia flowers, aloes, cornstalks, cyclamen, fenugreek, frankincense, heather, hollyhock, myrtle, oak leaves, sunflower, and wheat.

The traditional herbal incenses burned on this Sabbat are aloes, rose, and sandalwood.

Bilberries, stems of grain, and red poppies are appropriate altar decorations, as are seasonal flowers. Many covens decorate their Lammas altars with corn dollies (which are small figures fashioned from braided straw), while some prefer to use kirn babies (corn cob dolls). Both symbolize the Mother Goddess of the harvest.

Autumn Equinox

The Autumn Equinox Sabbat is celebrated by Wiccans on the first day of Fall. It is one of the four Minor (or Lesser) Sabbats celebrated each year and is also known as the Fall Sabbat, Alban Elfed, and the Second Festival of Harvest.

The traditional ritual herbs of the Autumn Equinox Sabbat are acorns, asters, benzoin, ferns, honeysuckle, marigold, milkweed, mums, myrrh, oak leaves, passionflower, pine, roses, sage, Solomon's seal, and thistles.

The traditional herbal incenses burned on this Sabbat are benzoin, myrrh, and sage.

Pomegranates symbolize the goddess Demeter's descent into the Underworld, and many covens who honor her on this day use these red fruits to decorate their Autumn

Equinox altars. Other traditional Pagan altar decorations for this Sabbat include acorns, pinecones, an ear of wheat (or other cereal crop), red poppies, and all autumnal flowers, leaves, and fruits.

Samhain

The Samhain Sabbat is celebrated by Wiccans on the thirty-first day of October. It is one of the four Major (or Grand) Sabbats celebrated each year and is also known as Halloween, Hallowmas, All Hallows' Eve, All Saints' Eve, Festival of the Dead, Calangaeaf, and the Third Festival of Harvest.

The traditional ritual herbs of the Samhain Sabbat are acorns, apples, broom, deadly nightshade, dittany of Crete, ferns, flax, fumitory, heather, mandrake, mullein, oak leaves, sage, and straw.

The traditional herbal incenses burned on this Sabbat are apple, heliotrope, mint, nutmeg, and sage.

Apples, which are traditionally used in Samhain divinations, are placed on the altar and around the circle on this "Witchiest" of all Sabbats. The carving of pumpkins into jack-o'-lanterns is also an ancient Pagan custom associated with this Sabbat. Many covens place one containing an orange or black candle at each of the four directional points of the circumference of the circle. Homemade herbal candles scented with apple or mint are used by some Wiccans as Samhain altar candles or to light the jack-o'-lanterns.

Winter Solstice

The Winter Solstice Sabbat is celebrated by Wiccans on the first day of Winter. It is one of the four Minor (or Lesser) Sabbats celebrated each year and is also known as

Yule, Winter Rite, Midwinter, and Alban Arthan.

The traditional ritual herbs of the Winter Solstice Sabbat are bay, bayberry, blessed thistle, cedar, chamomile, evergreen, frankincense, holly, juniper, mistletoe, moss, oak, pinecones, rosemary, and sage.

The traditional herbal incenses burned on this Sabbat are bayberry, cedar, pine, and rosemary.

The burning of an oak Yule log is a Pagan religious custom associated with the Winter Solstice since ancient times. Traditional herbal decorations for the Sabbat altar and circle include bayberries, holly, mistletoe, poinsettias, and a sprig of evergreen.

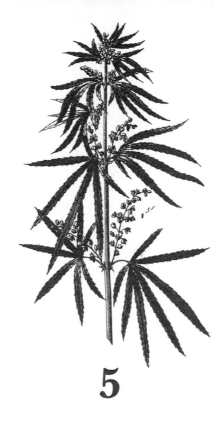

5

Mind-Altering Plants

The use of hallucinogenic plants as religious sacraments is an ancient custom practiced throughout the world by various cultures.

The religious use of mind-altering herbs is strongly discouraged in modern Wicca and Western high-magick tradition; however, in the Middle Ages they were commonly used by Witches and Wizards in flying ointments, love philtres, and magickal poisons.

Since the dawn of time, many shamans, visionaries,

medicine men, and other followers of various Pagan paths have eaten or smoked herbs possessing hallucinogenic properties in order to commune with God/Goddess, spirit beings, and extraterrestrial life forms; discover the purpose of life; divine the future; master astral projection; undergo a spiritual initiation; and achieve or duplicate mystical experiences.

This chapter neither promotes nor condemns the religious use of hallucinogenic plants; however, the reader should be advised that the possession and use of many of them are illegal in the United States as well as in other parts of the world. It is also important to bear in mind that extreme caution should be exercised whenever using herbs of this nature, because many of them are poisonous and can cause sickness or death.

One of the most popular mind-altering religious plants is the peyote, which is used in the traditional ceremonies of the Native American Church (and other groups) and is the subject of an ongoing legal controversy in the United States.

Peyote is a succulent spineless cactus which is native to the arid regions of Mexico, southern Texas, and Central America.

From the accounts of Spanish missionaries, the ceremonial use of peyote by Indian tribes of northern Mexico dates back to the sixteenth century. Its use spread rapidly to the tribes of North America after it was discovered across the border by the Comanche and Kiowa.

As a magickal and sacred plant, peyote has been used by over thirty Native American tribes from Saskatchewan to Mexico for clairvoyance, inducing religious visions, prophesying, healing, giving courage in warfare, and finding lost objects. It is astrologically ruled by the planets Mars and Saturn and is sacred to Peyote Woman, the Native American goddess who presides over the peyote cactus. It is also sacred to the fire god ("Grandfather"), earth goddess ("Grandmother"), and sun god ("Father") of the Huicholes tribe of the Sierra Madre Occidental.

According to an ancient Native American myth, the mystical properties of the peyote cactus were discovered by an Indian warrior who was lost in the desert and weak from a lack of food and water. His strength was miraculously revived and he was able to find his way back to his tribe after an inner voice, perhaps the voice of the peyote goddess, prompted him to eat some of the plant's mescal buttons.

The peyote cactus from which the drug mescaline is derived possesses cardiac, emetic, hallucinogenic, and narcotic properties. It is also believed to possess aphrodisiac qualities and the ability to promote the healing of scalp diseases. (**Warning**: Peyote often causes nausea and vomiting. Use it with extreme care and only under the supervision of one who is familiar with it!)

It is known as both "the sacred mushroom" and "the devil's root" (a name coined by the missionaries who condemned the cactus and zealously attempted to suppress its use in Native American rituals.)

Carlos Castaneda, the anthropologist and book author who was instructed by the Yaqui Indian brujo Don Juan Matus in the use of peyote, claims that one who uses peyote may encounter a personification of the plant (a spiritual entity known as Mescalito) who exists in reality as an independent power and uses the peyote cactus merely as his agent.

At one time it was a common belief among Indians that the peyote cactus was a deity or a messenger of the gods sent to communicate directly with a mortal without the medium of a holy man. Today many Native Americans still share these same beliefs as did their ancestors before them.

Jimsonweed (*Datura stramonium*) is a foul-smelling plant with prickly fruit and large, trumpet-shaped flowers of white, light blue, or purple that bloom from May through August.

It is believed that at the shrine of Apollo in the ancient Greek city of Delphi, the oracular priests were under the mind-altering influence and inspiration of jimsonweed smoke when they transmitted their prophecies.

In the first century, jimsonweed was introduced to Europe by the migrating Gypsies from India who smoked it to attain divinatory powers. It soon after became associated with Witchcraft and black magick, and in the medieval era it was one of the favorite (and deadliest) herbal poisons used by sorcerers and sorceresses to do away with enemies or rivals.

Jimsonweed is used by the Yaqui Indians of northern Mexico as a flying ointment, and by witch doctors in Togo as a highly magickal herb of divination to determine guilt or innocence.

In Peru the Quechua Indians also used jimsonweed as a tool of divination, believing that a man or woman under the plant's influence had the power to find their ancestral tombs, communicate with the dead, and foresee the future.

In the southwestern United States, jimsonweed was used by many Native American medicine men and shamans during ancient healing and fertility rituals. It was also regarded as a sacred herb in their rites of puberty, and as a potent female aphrodisiac.

Warning: Jimsonweed is an extremely dangerous plant, and it should never be taken internally. The seeds are hallucinogenic and may cause symptoms such as blurred vision (which can last over a week), the inability to urinate, dry mouth, irregular heartbeat, elevated blood pressure, fever, dilated pupils, headache, convulsions and coma. **An overdose of jimsonweed generally results in death.**

The leaves and berries of the bay laurel tree are said to possess excitant and narcotic properties and were used by the oracular priestesses of Delphi, who held bay leaves between their lips as they made their prophecies. As part of their sacred rituals, they would intoxicate themselves with bay potions that enabled them to enter trancelike states of consciousness in which they communicated directly with the gods (particularly Apollo), received visions, and prophesied.

Coca leaves (which produce the alkaloid crystal known as cocaine) and the hallucinogenic seeds of the morning glory plant (sacred to the Mother Goddess) are used by many Indian shamans of Mexico and South America to induce religious visions and to give them the powers of prophecy and divination.

While the possession and the religious use of morning glory seeds are not illegal in the United States, the reader should be aware that they contain D-lysergic acid amide and ergometrine, producing LSD-like experiences which can last up to six hours. (**Warning**: Pregnant women and persons suffering from hepatitis or other disorders of the liver should avoid eating morning glory seeds. In addition, some seed suppliers have been known to use a chemical called methyl mercury to treat the seeds in order to prevent them from spoiling. If ingested, this toxin can cause vomiting and diarrhea.)

The Mixtec Indian tribe of Mexico eat puffballs (a fungus of the genus *Lycoperdon*) before communicating with the spirit world. They believed that puffballs are sacred and highly magickal plants and that ingesting them can enable one to hear the voices of heaven.

The Algonquin Indian tribes of North America used a drug known as wysoccan, from the plant of the same name, in many of their religious ceremonies. This drug, which induces severe mental disorder and memory loss, would be taken by young men as part of their traditional rites of manhood so that all memories of boyhood could be erased from their minds.

In West Africa the dried bark of the tropical yohimbe tree is sniffed by tribal witch doctors to induce religious visions and to enable them to communicate with gods and supernatural beings of the spirit world. Yohimbe is also valued as a potent sex stimulant for men and is used in fertility rituals, love potions, and the sacred rites of sex magick.

Although yohimbe may be renowned for its "miraculous" aphrodisiac qualities, it also has its negative side. It may be unsafe for diabetics or persons who suffer from nervous disorders, schizophrenia, hypotension, or any disease of the heart, liver, or kidneys.

Yohimbine, a drug extracted from the tree's bark, has been reported to cause anxiety and sometimes psychosis and is considered to be an unsafe drug by the Food and Drug Administration. Additionally, recent medical studies have found that if taken in large quantities or over extended periods of time, it may cause temporary impotence to occur in some men.

In the Middle Ages, a dangerous herbal concoction producing psychedelic effects was said to be used by Witches for flying, shapeshifting, and even mastering invisibility. It was called "Witches' Flying Ointment" and consisted mainly of parsley, hemlock, water of aconite, poplar leaves, soot, bat's blood, deadly nightshade (or belladonna), henbane, and hashish.

In a large cauldron over a fire, these ingredients would be mixed together with (supposedly) the melted fat of an unbaptized infant and then rubbed on various parts of the Witch's body.

After being absorbed through the skin, the notorious flying ointments would produce vivid hallucinations, convulsions, and weird sensations of flying or leaving the body.

The opium poppy (*Papaver somniferum*) is a plant with grayish-green leaves and variously colored flowers. It is originally from Asia Minor and is the source of the drugs opium, morphine, codeine, and heroin, which are derived from the dried juice of the plant's unripe seed pods. (The poppy seeds themselves possess no psychoactive properties and are culinarily used mainly to season breads and rolls.)

The opium poppy was a sacred plant in India, and the smoking of opium was a religious practice associated with meditation and healing. In various parts of the world, opium potions that induced deep sleep were used by shamans who practiced dream magick. While in an opium sleep, spirit communications could be made, visions of the future revealed, and so forth.

The opium poppy is sacred to Hypnos (the Greek god of sleep) as well as to all Pagan deities of death and night. Around 1400 B.C., a benevolent deity known as the Poppy Goddess was worshipped by the women of Crete.

The Bureau of Narcotics in Washington, D.C., requires that a special permit be obtained by any person who plans to grow the opium poppy or any species or variety of poppy from which opium can be extracted. This comes under the Poppy Control Act of 1942.

Warning: Habitual use of opium can lead to strong addiction, and excessive use can result in serious health problems, coma, and death.

In ancient Greece, the poisonous and narcotic henbane (*Hyoscyamus niger*) was used by diviners as a magickal herb to induce visions of the future. As an herb of the sorcerer's art, it was used in love spells, weatherworking (to attract rain), flying ointments, shapeshifting ointments, and magickal poisons.

Numerous Native American tribes have used the hallucinogenic beans of the mescal-bean tree for religious purposes. During a centuries-old ceremony known as the Red Bean Dance, medicine men would dance, enter a trancelike state, and communicate with spirits while under the influence of mescal, and the visions which it produced in their minds were used to divine the future.

By the end of the nineteenth century, the place of mescal beans in Native American ceremonies was taken by peyote, which was safer to use and produced more colorful visions.

The hallucinogenic San Pedro cactus (*Trichocereus pachanoi*), which contains mescaline, has been used by shamans and folk healers in South America since ancient times. (Archeologists recently discovered a stone carving from 1300 B.C. which depicts an ancient god holding the sacred cactus in his hand.) The cactus is traditionally made into a potion which is then used, along with special prayers, invocations, and chants, in rituals of divination.

In the first century A.D., hemp (cannabis, marijuana) was used by the Chinese as a sacrament for achieving immortality and enabling one to see spirits. In India, where it was considered one of the country's five sacred plants, it was dedicated to the goddess Kali. Bhang (a drink made from the plant's leaves) was connected with the ancient Indian rites of sex magick.

Marijuana is ritually used by the Rastafarian sect of Jamaica, and hashish (a purified extract prepared from the dried flowers of the hemp plant) is smoked in the ceremonies of a religious cult in Arabia.

In various parts of Europe, hemp seeds were believed to bring good luck and were used traditionally at wedding ceremonies, Yule festivals, and initiation ceremonies. Ukrainian folklore holds that hemp seeds gathered on Saint John's Eve can magickally protect a person against all forms of evil.

Wild lettuce was used by certain Native American tribes as a sacrament for dream magick, and by Indian mystics for spiritual cleansing rituals known as *shank prakshalana*. When smoked prior to sleep, this herb enhances the vividness of dreams. (**Warning**: Wild lettuce should not be taken internally by any person who is affected with disorders of the stomach, such as ulcers. The use of this plant also slows the digestive process and impairs the sex drive.)

The worship of the sacred mushroom dates back to 300 A.D. It is known as "the flesh of the gods" and is connected with phallic worship, sex-magick rituals, and prophecy.

In Mexico, psilocybe mushrooms (which were sacred to the Aztecs) are ingested by men and women during Love Feasts in order to experience inner ecstasy. The Mazatec Indians ritually use this sacred mushroom in their divinatory curing rites and spirit communications, and the Mexican *curanderos*, or medicine men, value it for its ability to induce prophetic visions. "Magic mushrooms" (as they are often called) were also used by the followers of the ancient cults of Bacchus and Dionysus to achieve God-inspired frenzy. (**Warning**: Psilocybe mushrooms should not be used by pregnant women or any person who suffers from respiratory problems.)

The fly agaric (also known as "fly amanita") is a toxic mushroom, native to North America, Europe, and Asia. Although it usually has a red or orange cap with white wartlike patches, it can be found in other colors such as light brown, yellow, or white. Its name derives from its use as a flypaper poison.

Since early times this mushroom has been used in Siberia and by a few American Indian tribes along the Pacific Coast as an orgiastic and shamanistic inebriant. In the Indus Valley in India, the fly agaric was deified and worshipped by the Aryan people who followed the ancient cult of Soma. Extracts of the mushroom were used in initiation ceremonies, fertility rites, and religious rituals to draw down magickal powers from the heavens as well as to facilitate the growth of the spiritual body. (**Warning**: Fly agaric is very poisonous and it can cause **death** if ingested incorrectly.)

Galangal root is a hallucinogenic sacrament used by native peoples in the country of New Guinea. Throughout the world, it is valued as both a condiment and a folk medicine, as well as an herb to induce religious visions. In Asia, sorcerers eat the root in order to facilitate their magickal and psychic powers.

The formula for Aleister Crowley's incense of Abremelin contains galangal, which is used in a ritual that enables the magician to communicate with and receive knowledge from his (or her) holy guardian angel.

The following is an alphabetical listing of many of the plants discussed in this chapter, followed immediately by their botanical names and folk names (if known):

Aconite (*Aconitum napellus*), also known as Cupid's ear, dumbledore's delight, leopard's bane, monkshood, storm hat, Thor's hat, wolfbane, wolf's bane, and wolf's hat.

Bay Laurel (*Laurus nobilis*), also known as bay tree, Daphne, Grecian laurel, laurel, noble laurel, Roman laurel, and sweet bay.

Coca Shrub or Coca Plant (*Erythroxylum coca*).

Deadly Nightshade (*Atropa belladonna*), also known as banewort, belladonna, Death's herb, Devil's cherries, divale, dwale, dwaleberry, fair lady, great morel, naughty man's cherries, sorcerer's berry, and Witch's berry.

Fly Agaric (*Amanita muscaria*), also known as amrita, death angel, death cap, magic mushroom, pank, porg, redcap, and sacred mushroom.

Galangal Root (*Alpinia officinarum*), also known as catarrh root, chewing John, China root, colic root, India root, Low John the Conqueror, and maraba.

Hemlock (*Conium maculatum*), also known as beaver poison, Herb Bennet, keckies, kex, musquash root, poison hemlock, poison parsley, spotted corobane, spotted hemlock, warlock weed, and water parsley.

Hemp (*Cannabis sativa*), also known by numerous nicknames, including bhang, dope, gage, gallowgrass, ganja, grass, kif, marijuana, neckweed, Mary Jane, pot, tea, and weed.

Henbane (*Hyoscyamus niger*), also known as black nightshade, cassilago, cassilata, Devil's eye, hebenor, henbells, hogsbean, isana, Jupiter's bean, poison tobacco, and symphonica.

Jimsonweed (*Datura stramonium*), also known as angel's trumpet, Devil's apple, Gabriel's trumpet, ghost flower, Jamestown weed, love-will, mad apple, mad herb, manicon, sorcerer's herb, stinkweed, thorn apple, yerba del diablo (which translates to "herb of the Devil"), and Witch's thimble.

Mescal Bean Tree (*Sophora secundiflora*), also known as dream seeds, red beans, and oracle beans.

Morning Glory (*Ipomoea violacea*), also known as bindweed, blue stars, flying saucers, heavenly blue, and pearly gates.

Opium Poppy (*Papaver somniferum*), which translates to "the poppy that brings sleep"), also known as blind buff, blind eyes, headaches, and head waak.

Peyote (*Lophophora williamsii*), also known as Devil's root, mescal buttons, and sacred mushroom.

Poplar (*Populus tremuloides*).

Psilocybe Mushroom (*Psilocybe baeocystis*), also known as cultivator's cap, elf's stool, flesh of the gods, liberty cap, magic mushroom, and strophana.

Puffball (Genus *Lycoperdon*).

San Pedro Cactus (*Trichocereus pachanoi*).

Wild Lettuce (*Lactuca virosa*), also known as compass plant, horse thistle, lettuce opium, lopium, prickly lettuce, and wild opium.

Yohimbe (*Corynanthe yohimbe*).

6

The Magickal Mandrake

The mandrake is a poisonous narcotic plant associated with medieval Witchcraft and sorcery and is believed to be the most magickal of all plants and herbs. It is ruled by the planet Venus (or Mercury) and is potent in all forms of enchantment.

Mandrake, whose botanical name is *Mandragora officnarum*, is a native of the Mediterranean region. Its name means "man-dragon."

It is a close relative to the nightshade family, having

purplish or greenish-yellow flowers, berries that seem to glow phosphorescently at sunrise, and a thick branched root that resembles the human body or a phallus. The flowers of this stemless perennial herb possess a strong and unpleasant smell, and from its unusual root a narcotic was formerly prepared.

In the ancient days of the Greeks and Romans, the juice of the root was used medicinally as an anesthetic prior to performing surgeries and cauterizations on patients.

Caution should always be exercised when using any part of the mandrake in potions, brews, and philtres. It is a highly toxic plant, and misuse of it can result in sickness, delirium, or a slow and agonizing death.

Authentic European mandrake is extremely difficult to find in North America and quite expensive to buy. The "mandrake" sold at many occult supply stores and herbal shops in the United States is actually a plant called the mayapple (*Podophyllum peltatum*), which is a native of North America and in no way related to the European mandrake.

The mayapple (or "American mandrake," as it is often called) possesses a single, nodding white flower and oval yellow fruit. Although the pulp of the ripe fruit is edible, the roots, leaves, and seeds of the "American mandrake" are just as deadly as its European counterpart.

It is said that there are female mandrake roots in addition to male ones. The female ones are often called "woman-drakes" and are shaped like the body of a woman, just as the male mandrake roots are in the shape of a man's.

Both are equally as powerful as far as their powers of magick are concerned; however, many Witches of the female gender prefer to work with the female mandrakes, especially when spells dealing with love and sexuality are involved.

The mandrake root is the most powerful herb of love

magick, and certainly one of the most deadliest. Ones that resemble a phallus are believed to possess great aphrodisiac qualities and were, at one time, the main ingredient used in Witches' love philtres (potions) despite their highly toxic properties.

According to Pliny the Elder, "When a mandrake root in the shape of a male genital organ was found, it secured genital love."

In the Orient, mandrake roots are commonly sold in herbal shops and drugstores as a sex stimulant. They can be bought either whole or in powdered form, and usually at an exorbitant price.

A mandrake root that is soaked every Friday in a bowl of white wine and then carried in a charm bag made of red silk and velvet will give its possessor great sexual potency and make him or her attractive to the opposite sex.

A mandrake root placed underneath a bed pillow will arouse passion between two lovers, even if one is indifferent.

In the Arab nations, many men who suffer from declining sexual potency wear a mandrake root on a necklace as a virility-enhancing amulet.

Female fertility is also promoted by eating mandrake (especially the female of the roots) or by carrying one as a charm, according to legend. It has been used for centuries by women who desired large families and also by those who wanted to bear male children.

In the book of Genesis, Joseph was said to have been conceived after Rachel (Jacob's wife who suffered from "barreness") ate a mandrake root. This clearly traces the belief in mandrake as a fertility charm back to biblical times.

According to folklore, the fruit of the mandrake (known in some cultures as "love apples") can cause a man to fall in love with a woman if she gives it to him on Saint Agnes's Eve (January 20).

A tiny particle of powdered female mandrake leaf added to a cup of red wine (for "passionate lovemaking") or white wine (for "romantic love") is said to be a powerful Witch's aphrodisiac.

In addition to love magick, mandrake roots have long been believed to possess the power to divine the future. More than one book on medieval Witchcraft and sorcery states that the human-shaped roots (both male and female) shake their heads to answer yes or no when questions are put to them. With the proper incantations, mandrakes can also be made to speak out loud or through telepathy. This is another way in which they can prophesy the future and reveal secrets.

According to one "old wives' tale," if a mandrake root takes a liking to a novice magician, it will teach him (or her) the highly sought-after secrets of the magickal arts.

Mandrakes have been used by many modern Witches in spells and rituals that increase the psychic powers. They are carried in mojo bags or worn on necklaces as powerful charms to attract good luck, and it is said that money placed in a box with a mandrake root will double overnight.

In medieval times it was widely believed that special ointments containing powdered mandrake root were used by Witches. These ointments, which were given the nickname of "sorcerer's grease," supposedly enabled Witches to fly, become invisible, or magickally transform themselves into animals and birds when they were rubbed onto the body. Of course, Witches never did actually fly, become invisible, or shapeshift; however, the wild visions and sensations produced when the hallucinogenic ointments were absorbed into the skin more than likely led them to believe that they had.

In the country of Arabia, mandrake is called the "Devil's candle" or "Devil's light." These nicknames derive from the old folk belief that the plant's leaves glow in the dark, a phenomenon produced by glowworms, according to one source.

The mandrake has, over the centuries and in various parts of the world, been given many other nicknames, including "man-dragon," "warlock root," "earth-man-ikin," "root of evil," and the "little gallows-man." (The latter derives from the medieval legend that the mandrake grows under a gallows tree from the blood or other bodily fluids of hanged criminals who were unbaptized or born with evil blood in their veins.)

Mandrake roots should be uprooted from the earth only at night (especially when the Moon is full) and always by the magician who intends to use it, otherwise the root's magickal powers are rendered useless.

Another legend tells us that a mandrake root shrinks whenever a man or woman approaches it, unless, of course, that person happens to be a Witch, a Wizard, or someone who is in league with the Devil.

Mandrake is one of the traditional ritual herbs of the Samhain (Halloween) Witches' Sabbat and is sacred to the following Pagan deities: Aphrodite, Diana, Hecate, and the legendary Teutonic sorceress known as the Alrauna Maiden.

Legend of the Screaming Mandrake

A medieval legend claims that when a mandrake plant is uprooted, it emits an ear-piercing scream and begins to sweat blood. The same legend also states that any man or woman who pulls the root from the earth is doomed to instantly suffer an agonizing death upon hearing the evil scream.

It is unknown how or where this interesting legend originated.

Many methods of safe mandrake harvesting were de-vised over the years by practitioners of sorcery and wizardry. The most popular method employed was as follows: First, the soil around the mandrake plant would be loosened with a shovel or other implement. Then one end of a rope would be tied around a dog's neck and the other to the plant. The dog's master (who places cotton inside his ears to protect himself against the plant's deadly shriek) would then walk some distance away and command the dog to come to him or offer it some food. As the dog ran to its master, the mandrake root was pulled out from the ground by the rope. The dog would be instantly killed by the evil scream; however, the animal's death was believed to give the root of the mandrake the supernatural power to protect its possessor against demonic entities.

Circe's Plant

In Homer's second epic, the *Odyssey*, an enchantress by the name of Circe was said to have used a magickal potion made from the juice of the mandrake root to first inflame Odysseus' men with love and then turn them into swine.

It was also from the mandrake that she concocted a powerful magickal poison that transformed the fair water-nymph Scylla into a grotesque and dangerous six-headed sea monster who despised and destroyed everything that came within her reach.

The ancient Greeks called the mandrake "Circe's plant" and dedicated it to this beautiful but deadly Witch-goddess of the island of Aeaea.

It has been associated with Witches and the magickal arts ever since.

Mandragoras

The term "mandragora" is used by herbalists for the narcotic prepared from the mandrake. At one time it was a word also used by poets to mean the entire mandrake plant; however, it has fallen out of use in modern times.

In folklore the name "mandragora" is given to a type of spirit or demon associated with the mandrake plant, in particular the human-shaped root.

These supernatural beings are said to take the form of tiny, beardless men with black-colored skin. They roam secretly among the human population, often causing mischief, and are summoned by sorcerers whom they assist in the practice of black magick.

Some mandragoras inhabit the roots of mandrake plants when not busy aiding magicians or amusing themselves by wreaking havoc on the mortal race. Some mandragoras transform themselves into mandrakes, and others remain invisible but can be conjured with a special incantation recited over a mandrake root.

Curiously, while these spirits or demons are capable of inhabiting or changing into a mandrake root of either sex, the mandragora always remains of the male gender.

Belief in mandragoras and their magickal powers was common in Germany and Arabia throughout the Middle Ages. Many believed that these strange beings could bring on madness to any man or beast if that was the will of the sorcerer who conjured them. Numerous charms and amulets were employed for protection against them.

During the "burning times," mandragoras were believed to have been the imps or demon familiars of Witches and Warlocks, along with the more traditional cats and toads. A mandrake root in one's possession was certain proof of sorcery to Witch-hunters, and could easily cost any woman, man, or child (Witch or not) their life.

Growing Your Own Mandrake

For a bit of homegrown magick (and also to save yourself some money by not having to pay high prices for mandrake at herb and occult shops), try planting a Witch's mandrake garden, or add this mystical plant to an existing herb or flower garden in your backyard.

European mandrake, which is propagated by seed or root division, should be planted in the center of small mounds of soil about twelve inches apart, and grows well when planted alone or next to aconite (*Aconitum napellus*) or Echinacea (*Echinacea augustifolia*).

Zone Seven of the United States Department of Agriculture's plant hardiness zone map (average minimum temperature of 0 to 10 degrees Fahrenheit) is the ideal climate for mandrake to grow in.

Like most perennial plants, mandrake prefers full sunshine or partial shade, good soil, and proper drainage.

Seed planting or root division should be done in early Spring and when the Moon is full and/or in the astrological sign of Taurus, Capricorn, Pisces, Cancer, Scorpio, or Libra. Do not plant when the Moon is in its waning phase or in one of the Barren Signs: Leo, Gemini, Virgo, Sagittarius, Aquarius, or Aries.

In late Spring, the mandrake blooms with greenish-yellow flowers that grow in the shape of bells, approximately one inch long. Its leaves have a wrinkled appearance and grow to be about twelve inches in length.

The mandrake is not considered to be an ornamental plant, and in days of old it was grown only in the medicinal garden by folk healers and Witchy-women who used its root as a painkiller and a sedative.

I do not under any circumstances recommend that you use mandrake for medicinal purposes of any kind, as all parts of the plant are **highly toxic**. Mandrake should be grown only for magickal or religious use, and certainly not in an area where children or pets could have access to it and possibly ingest it.

Mandrake can also be grown indoors in a flowerpot large enough to accommodate a foot-tall plant. Keep it near a sunny window (preferably one with a southern exposure), talk to it often, and give it some water once or twice a week.

Male and female mandrake roots. (Woodcut from the *Hortus Sanitatis*. Augsburg 1486.)

7

Herbs of the Divinatory Arts

Herbs of Divination

Divination is the ancient science, art, and practice of discovering the unknown and foretelling events of the future by interpreting omens or by various occult methods.

The divinatory arts have always been associated with

Witches, Wizards, and the Old Religion, and its practice (both past and present) is universal.

Plants and trees, with their wealth of occult lore and magickal associations, have long been interpreted for omens, used to induce prophetic dreams, and ritually smoked or ingested to give a person the ability of soothsaying or second sight.

Like Goddess worship and the magickal arts, divination is an important facet of Wicca. It is not only used by Wiccans for foretelling future events and locating lost or hidden objects, but more importantly to find out if a particular spell is necessary and also to discover whether the results of it will have a positive or negative effect. This is important to Wiccans so that they don't (even through well-meaning intentions or by accident) violate the Threefold Law. (To those of you who are unfamiliar with the nature-oriented religion of Wicca, this is the belief that if a Witch uses white magick or positive energy to do something good for somebody else, he or she will get it back threefold in the same lifetime. By the same token, if a Witch uses black magick or negative energy to bring harm unto others, it is also returned to him or her threefold in the same lifetime.)

The Threefold Law, which is also known as Triple Karma, walks hand in hand with the Wiccan Rede—a simple and benevolent moral code of Wiccans that is as follows: "An it harm none, do what thou wilt." The Wiccan Rede is extremely important to bear in mind before performing any magickal spells or rituals, especially those which may be considered unethical or of a manipulative nature.

The herb yarrow is associated with the ancient Chinese system of oracular divination known as the I Ching (or "Book of Changes"). Although the modern and most common method of consulting the I Ching is to toss three coins three times to randomly determine hexagrams, the traditional (and more complicated) method is to toss fifty sticks of yarrow and then interpret the hexagrams produced.

Another ancient method of divination popular in the country of China involves bamboo (the emblem of the sacred fire, and a plant long associated with Moon worship and lunar magick). Temple priests look into the future and the unknown by throwing pieces of bamboo to a worshipper and then drawing significant omens from the way in which the wood falls.

According to folklore, a dandelion can tell a person how long he or she will live. This is done by blowing the seeds off the dandelion's head and then counting the remaining ones. The total number of seeds left will equal the number of years you will live.

To aid divination, many Witches burn bistort with frankincense in an incense burner prior to scrying. Camphor is also used in divinatory incenses and is said to be very potent in stimulating the third-eye chakra.

It was once believed that drinking a magickal potion made of buchu leaves could give a man or woman the supernatural power to look into the future. The same was said of infusions of broom; however, this is a very poisonous plant and ingesting it is not recommended!

Mugwort is brewed as a tea, often with lemon balm, and consumed to aid divination (as well as meditation and psychic development). Mugwort tea is also used by Witches and scryers as a wash to cleanse and consecrate divination tools such as crystal balls, magic mirrors, and quartz crystals.

The leaves of the fig tree can be used to answer yes or no to questions or to determine good or bad omens. If a fig leaf upon which a question has been written takes a long time to dry, it indicates a yes answer or a good omen. A fig leaf that dries up rapidly indicates a negative answer or a bad omen.

The seeds of an apple or orange are also used by many

Witches to answer yes or no to a question. After writing your question on the peel of the fruit, cut it open with an athame and count the number of seeds contained within it. If they add up to an odd number, it indicates a yes answer; a no if the number of seeds are even.

In addition to answering yes-or-no questions, seeds can also reveal other things, such as the number of children one will have in the future. In certain parts of the world, women have employed the fruit of the pomegranate for this purpose. After asking it to tell them how many children they will be blessed with, they throw it hard on the ground and then count the number of seeds that fall out of it. This number is then interpreted as the answer to their question.

The hibiscus is a popular divination flower among many islanders of the Western Pacific. To see into the future, sorcerers put several hibiscus flowers into a wooden bowl filled with sea water and then gaze into it until they enter a vision-producing trancelike state.

If you suspect that someone is using black magick to harm you in any way, you can find out who the perpetrator is by placing some ground ivy around a yellow candle and burning it on the third day of the week (Tuesday). If you concentrate hard enough, the guilty sorcerer or sorceress will appear in your mind's eye.

Meadowsweet gathered on Saint John's Day (Midsummer) can magickally tell you the gender of a thief when it is placed on water. If the meadowsweet floats, it is an indication that the thief is female; if it sinks, it means a man is the culprit.

Goldenrod is said to enable a Witch to find buried treasure or things that are lost or hidden from view. If you are right-handed, hold a goldenrod in your left hand. If you are left-handed, hold it in your right hand. Ask it to show you where the object is and the flower will point you in the right direction.

An orris root suspended from a piece of yarn is used by many as an effective dowsing pendulum, especially when the Moon is positioned in the astrological sign of Venus.

Trees Associated With Dowsing

Dowsing (or water-witching) is the ancient occult art of locating subterranean water or buried objects by holding a forked stick or branch that twitches and bends downward when held over the source.

The sticks used by dowsers are called divining rods, and they are traditionally made from the forked twigs of the hazel (a tree with a long reputation of possessing potent magickal properties).

Wands of hazel were mentioned in the ancient writings of the Roman scholar Pliny as tools for divining underground springs. They are also believed by many to be able to locate metals, criminals, missing animals, and buried treasure as well.

Other woods that are often employed by dowsers are ash, blackthorn (or sloe), rowan, and willow. These are said by many to work just as well as hazel. According to one book on magickal herbs, a branch of pomegranate works especially well for dowsers who wish to locate concealed money.

The art of dowsing is believed to be over seven thousand years old and was practiced extensively throughout ancient Egypt and China.

Herbs of Love Divination

The daisy is used in what is perhaps the most popular and well-known form of love divination, commonly practiced by children and young teens in England and the United States. To determine whether or not the love of your boyfriend (or girlfriend) is true, pluck the petals from a daisy while repeating the famous words: "He loves me. He loves me not."

The daisy is also used in another method of love divination to determine how many years will pass before you get married. Pluck a handful of grass and daisies with your eyes closed, and the number of daisies that you find in the bunch will indicate the number of years.

If you cannot decide between two lovers, scratch the name of each man or woman on a separate onion. Leave the onions in a warm place and the one that sprouts first will denote the more passionate love.

To find out how many years will pass before you wed, according to old country lore of England, pick a dandelion and the number of puffs it takes for you to blow off all of its fuzzy seeds will indicate the number of years you must wait.

To test the fidelity of your lover, kneel beside your bed and twine together two rose stems. If the color of the roses begins to appear darker, it is a sign that your lover has been faithful to you. Another method of testing fidelity is as follows: Place a poppy petal on top of your left fist and then strike it with your right hand. If it makes a popping sound, it is a sign that your lover is true. If not, your love has not been a faithful one.

To predict a happy marriage, young men in the Orient pick a bachelor's button (cornflower) at dawn and carry it in their pocket for twenty-four hours. If the flower stays fresh, the marriage will be good; if the flower withers, the young man will soon find a new love.

To see an image of your future spouse, make a "Witch's chain" of juniper and mistletoe berries tied with acorns and wound around a branch. Cast the chain into a blazing hearthfire, and as the last acorn burns, a vision will come to you.

Love Dreams

One of the most popular methods of love divination practiced around the world is the prophetic love dream in which the dreamer sees the face of his or her future lover or marriage mate. To induce such a dream, one must place any of the following herbal charms under his or her pillow before going to sleep: wild yarrow plucked from a graveyard, nine female holly leaves wrapped in a three-cornered handkerchief tied with nine knots, daisy roots, an onion, a poplar branch tied with your socks or stockings, two laurel leaves, or ten ivy leaves gathered in silence on Halloween night.

Love-dream divination is traditionally performed on Saint Valentine's Day, Saint Agnes's Eve (the night of January 20), and Saint John's Eve (June 23, the night before Midsummer's Day, which is also a traditional time for Witches to gather herbs for spells and love potions. It is believed that the magickal properties of plants are greatest on this night.)

Apple Love Divination

To find out the initial of your future lover's name, peel an apple in one long, continuous strip and then toss the peel over your left shoulder. Whichever letter of the alphabet it forms will be the initial.

Twist the stem of an apple as you recite the letters of the alphabet and whichever letter you are on when the stem comes off will be the initial of your future lover's name. (If you reach the end of the alphabet, begin again at the letter A.)

To see the image of future husbands, medieval maidens would stand in front of a mirror with an apple, slice it into nine pieces, and impale each piece on the point of a knife, holding it over their left shoulders.

To find out who your future husband will be, take a bunch of apples and write the name of a potential suitor on each one. Place the apples over a blazing fire, and the person whose name is on the apple which pops first will be the one you will marry.

According to an old folk custom in Austria, if an apple cut on Saint Thomas's Eve (December 20) contains an even number of seeds, it indicates a wedding. If one of the seeds is cut in half, it foretells a troubled marriage. If two seeds are cut, it is an omen of widowhood.

8

Heavenly Herbs

Planetary Correspondences

In the Middle Ages, astrologically-minded herbalists (such as Nicholas Culpepper) strongly believed that the sun, moon, and planets of our solar system exerted a mystical influence over certain herbs. These influences were taken into consideration when herbs were planted or harvested, and also when they were used medicinally.

The following is a list of the planets, followed by the

many plants and trees which each one traditionally rules over:

Earth: acorns and mushrooms.

Jupiter: agrimony, alexander, alfalfa, arrowhead, arrowroot, asparagus, avens, balm, balm of Gilead, banyon tree, betony, bilberry, bladder wrack, blazing star, bo tree, boneset, borage, bugloss, cardamom, carnation, chervil, chestnut tree, chicory, cinquefoil, cloves, costmary, couch grass, currants, dandelion, dock, dog's grass, endive, fig tree, fir tree, hare's ear, henna, houseleek, hyacinth, jasmine, lime tree, liverwort, lungwort, magnolia tree, maple tree, milkweed, mistletoe, moneywort, mulberry tree, myrrh, nutmeg, oak tree, olive tree, peepul tree, plane tree, pleurisy root, rose hips, sage, samphire, sandalwood, scurvy grass, spinach, sumac tree, sweet cicely, sycamore tree, thistle (Our Lady's), thorn apple, Ti plant, and Witch grass.

Mars: acacia, all-heal, aloes, anemones, asparagus fern, barberry, basil, bearberry, brookweed, broom, bryony, cacti, cashew tree, cayenne, chili powder, chives, coriander, cranesbill, cress (black), crowfoot, cubebs, cuckoopint, cumin, furze, garlic, gentian, germander, hawthorn tree, honeysuckle, hops, horseradish, hyssop, juniper tree, leeks, lichen, lupine, madder, masterwort, mastic tree, mescal, mustard, nettles, onion, oregano, peppers, peyote, pilewort, plantain, radish, rhubarb, sarsaparilla, savin, snapdragon, spikenard, squill, tarragon, thistle (blessed), thistle (star), toadflax, tobacco, woodruff, and wormwood.

Mercury: agaric, alstonia, aspen tree, azalea, balsam tree, bayberry, bittersweet, buckwheat, calamint, caraway, carrots, cassia, cedar tree, celery, cinquefoil, coffee tree, cow parsnip, dill, dog's Mercury, elecampane, fennel, fenugreek, ferns, flax, germander, goat's rue, hare's foot, hazel tree, honeysuckle, horehound, Jacob's ladder, lady's slipper, lavender, licorice, lily of the valley, mandrake, marjoram, meadowsweet, mulberry tree, parsley, parsnips, pellitory, pomegranate tree, Queen Anne's lace, sarsaparilla, sassafras, savory, scabious, sedge, senna, southernwood, spurge, tea, valerian, wandering Jew.

Moon: acanthus, adder's tongue, African daisy, algae, anise, banana tree, cabbage, calla lily, chickweed, clary sage, colewort, cress (water), cucumber, dog rose, dog-tooth violet, duckweed, flag, fleur-de-lis, ginger, goose grass, iris, jasmine, lady's smock, loosestrife, mango tree, moonwort, mountain ash tree, mugwort, opium poppy, orach, orpine, orris root, pearl trefoil, privet, pumpkin, purslane, rose (white), rowan tree, rushes, sea holly, seaweed, sesame, stonecrop, sweet flag, wallflower, water chestnut, watercress, water lily, water mosses, willow tree, and wintergreen.

Neptune: Adam and Eve root, apricot tree, balmony, dogwood tree, hemp, jewelweed, lobelia, lotus, mescal, narcissus, orange tree, passionflower, peach tree, pear tree, soapwort, wisteria.

Pluto: agaric, asafetida, asphodel, bearberry, damiana, eucalyptus tree, foxglove, oats, patchouli, rye, unicorn root (false), wormwood, and yucca.

Saturn: aconite, amaranthus, arnica, barley, beech tree, beets, belladonna, bindweed, bird's-foot, bistort, bluebell, box tree, buckthorn, campion, carob, comfrey, cramp bark, crosswort, cypress tree, darnel, deadly nightshade, elm tree, fleawort, fumitory, goutwort, heart's ease, hellebore, hemlock tree, hemp, henbane, holly, horsetail, ilex, Irish moss, ivy, jimsonweed, knapweed, knot grass, marijuana, medlar tree, mescal, mezereon, monkshood, mosses, mullein, myrrh, pansy, peyote, pine tree, plumbago, poison hemlock, pokeweed, polypody, poplar tree, potato, quince tree, service tree, shepherd's purse, skullcap, snakeweed, Solomon's seal, spleenwort, tamarind tree, thistle (melancholy), Virginia creeper, wax plant, Witch hazel, woad, wolfsbane, woundwort, and yew tree.

Sun: almond tree, angelica, artichoke, ash tree, bay tree, bromeliads, burnet, butterbur, celandine, centaury, chamomile, cinnamon, daffodil, eyebright, frankincense, galangel, heliotrope, juniper tree, laurel tree, lovage, marigold, mayweed, mistletoe, olive tree, palm trees, peony, rice, rosemary, rue, saffron, Saint John's wort, saxifrage, scarlet pimpernel, storax tree, sundew, swallowwort, tormentil, vines, and walnut tree.

Uranus: allspice, chicory, coffee tree, elecampane, ginseng, kola tree, nutmeg tree, pomegranate tree, trailing arbutus, unicorn root (true).

Venus: African violet, ageratum, alder tree, amaryllis, apple tree, apricot tree, avocado tree, Aztec lily, balm of Gilead, beans, bergamot tree, birch tree, bishop's weed, blackberry, bloodroot, boneset, bramble, breadfruit tree, bugleweed, burdock, catnip, cherry tree, chickpea, clover, coconut tree, coltsfoot, columbines, cornflower, cotton rose, cottonweed, cowslip, crocus, cudweed, daisy, dead nettle, dittany, dogwood tree, dropwort, elder tree, eryngo, everlasting, feverfew, figwort, fleabane, foxglove, gardenia, geranium, goldenrod, goldenseal, gooseberry, ground ivy, groudsel, heather, herb Robert, hibiscus, hollyhock, jewelweed, kava-kava, kidneywort, lady's mantle, lady's bedstraw, lemongrass, lentil, lily of the valley, mallows, meadowsweet, mints, moneywort, motherwort, mugwort, myrtle tree, orange tree, orchid, passionflower, peach tree, pear tree, pennyroyal, peppermint, periwinkle, plane tree, plantain, plum tree, pomegranate

tree, primrose, ragweed, ragwort, rampion, rasp
rose (red), sage, sanicle, self-heal, soapwort, speec ..1,
strawberry, sycamore tree, tansy, teazles, thistle (sow),
toadflax, tulip, verbena, vervain, violets, winter cherry,
woodruff, wood sorrel, and yarrow.

Astrological Trees and Herbs

The following is a list of the twelve signs of the zodiac,
followed by some of the trees and herbs over which they
rule. (The trees and herbs influenced by a particular
astrological sign are said to be extremely lucky for all
persons who are born under that sign.)

Aries (ruled by the planets Mars and Pluto) is the first
sign of the zodiac, symbolized by the ram. Its gender is
masculine, and its element is fire. The trees and herbs
under the astrological influence of Aries are garlic, holly,
honeysuckle, rosemary, thistle, all thorn-bearing trees,
and thyme.

Taurus (ruled by the planet Venus) is the second sign of
the zodiac, symbolized by the bull. Its gender is feminine,
and its element is earth. The trees and herbs under the
astrological influence of Taurus are almond, ash, cypress,
foxglove, poppy, rose, vervain, vines, and violet.

Gemini (ruled by the planet Mercury) is the third sign of
the zodiac, symbolized by the twins. Its gender is masculine, and its element is air. The trees and herbs under
the astrological influence of Gemini are lavender, lily of
the valley, meadowsweet, mosses, all nut-bearing trees,
and tansy.

Cancer (ruled by the Moon) is the fourth sign of the
zodiac, symbolized by the crab. Its gender is feminine,

and its element is water. The trees and herbs under the astrological influence of Cancer are acanthus, adder's tongue, agrimony, jasmine, moonwort, all trees rich in sap, and all white flowers.

Leo (ruled by the Sun) is the fifth sign of the zodiac, symbolized by the lion. Its gender is masculine, and its element is fire. The trees and herbs under the astrological influence of Leo are angelica, bay laurel tree, marigold, palm trees, rue, saffron, sage, Saint John's wort, sunflower, and walnut tree.

Virgo (ruled by the planet Mercury) is the sixth sign of the zodiac, symbolized by the virgin. Its gender is feminine, and its element is earth. The trees and herbs under the astrological influence of Virgo are fennel, lavender, all nut-bearing trees, oats, rye, and small brightly colored flowers.

Libra (ruled by the planet Venus) is the seventh sign of the zodiac, symbolized by the scales, or balance. Its gender is masculine, and its element is air. The trees and herbs under the astrological influence of Libra are almond tree, ash tree, cypress, hydrangea, primrose, rose (white), strawberry, vines, and all blue flowers.

Scorpio (ruled by the planets Mars and Pluto) is the eighth sign of the zodiac, symbolized by the scorpion. Its gender is feminine, and its element is water. The trees and herbs under the astrological influence of Scorpio are basil, blackthorn, all bushy trees, geranium, ginseng, mustard, oregano, and all red flowers.

Sagittarius (ruled by the planet Jupiter) is the ninth sign of the zodiac, symbolized by the centaur-archer. Its gender is masculine, and its element is fire. The trees and herbs under the astrological influence of Sagittarius are ash tree, chestnut tree, dandelion, feverfew, mallows, oak tree, lime tree, birch tree, and all pink flowers.

Capricorn (ruled by the planet Saturn) is the tenth sign of the zodiac, symbolized by the goat or goat-fish (a mythological creature depicted as part goat and part fish). Its gender is feminine, and its element is earth. The trees and herbs under the astrological influence of Capricorn are aconite, belladonna, comfrey, elm tree, ivy, pansy, pine trees, poplar tree, and yew tree.

Aquarius (ruled by the planet Uranus) is the eleventh sign of the zodiac, symbolized by the water bearer. Its gender is masculine, and its element is air. The trees and herbs under the astrological influence of Aquarius are anise, frankincense, all fruit trees, myrrh, orchid, spikenard, and wisteria.

Pisces (ruled by the planets Neptune and Jupiter) is the twelfth sign of the zodiac, symbolized by the two fish. Its gender is feminine, and its element is water. The trees and herbs under the astrological influence of Pisces are hemp, seaweed, water lily, water mosses, white poppy, and willow tree.

Elemental Herbs

Each one of the four ancient and mystical elements of nature (Earth, Air, Fire, and Water) rules over a particular group of plants and trees, and are regarded in Western occultism as the basis of all life throughout the universe. They are linked with the four quarters of the magician's circle and form the foundation of natural magick.

The following is a list of the elements and the plants which are under their domain:

Earth (the element associated with the female principle

and the North cardinal point of the magick circle) is the ruler of alfalfa, asphodel, barley, bistort, buckwheat, corn, cotton, cypress, fern, fumitory, honeysuckle, horehound, horsetail, knotweed, loosestrife, magnolia, mugwort, oats, oleander, patchouli, primrose, quince, rhubarb, rye, sagebrush, tulip, turnip, vervain, vetivert, wheat, and wood sorrel.

Air (the element associated with the male principle and the East cardinal point of the magick circle) is the ruler of acacia, agrimony, almond, anise, aspen tree, banyan tree, bergamot, bittersweet, bodhi tree, borage, bracken, broom, clover, dandelion, dock, elecampane, endive, eyebright, fenugreek, goat's rue, goldenrod, hazel, hops, houseleek, lavender, lemongrass, lemon verbena, lily of the valley, linden, maple tree, marjoram, meadowsweet, mint, mistletoe, mulberry, palm, parsley, pimpernel, pine trees, sage, senna, slippery elm, southernwood, star anise, summer savory, and wax plant.

Water (the element associated with the female principle and the West cardinal point of the magick circle) is the ruler of alder tree, amaranth, angelica, ash tree, avens, basil, bay laurel tree, bloodroot, briony, cactus, carnation, cattail, cedar, celandine, celery, centaury, chrysanthemum, cinnamon, cinquefoil, clove, coriander, cubeb, cumin, damiana, deer's tongue, dill, fennel, fig tree, flax, frankincense, galangal, garlic, gentian, ginger, ginseng, goldenseal, grains of paradise, hawthorn tree, heliotrope, High John the Conqueror, holly, hyssop, juniper, lime tree, liverwort, lovage, mandrake (mandragora), marigold, masterwort, mayapple, mullein, mustard, nutmeg, oak tree, olive tree, onion, orange tree, pennyroyal, peppermint, pepper tree, pineapple tree, poke root, pomegranate, prickly gorse, radish, rosemary, rowan tree, rue, saffron, Saint John's wort, sarsaparilla, sassafras, snapdragon, squill, sunflower, thistle, Ti plant, toadflax, tobacco, tormentil, Venus flytrap, walnut tree, Witch hazel, wood betony, woodruff, wormwood, and yucca.

Fire (the element associated with the male principle and the South cardinal point of the magick circle) is the ruler of Adam and Eve root, African violet, aloe vera, althea, apple tree, apricot tree, aster, avocado, bachelor's buttons, balm of Gilead, banana tree, belladonna, birch tree, blackberry, bladderwrack, blue flag, boneset, buchu, buckthorn, burdock, cabbage, calamus, camelia, cardamon, catnip, chamomile, cherry tree, chickweed, club moss, coconut tree, coltsfoot, columbine, comfrey, cowslip, crocus, daffodil, daisy, datura, dittany of Crete, elder, elm tree, eryngo, eucalyptus, feverfew, foxglove, gardenia, grap, groundsel, heather, hellebore, hemlock, hemp, henbane, hibiscus, huckleberry, hyacinth, Indian paintbrush, iris, Irish moss, jasmine, jimsonweed, kava-kava, lady's bedstraw, lady's mantle, lady's slipper, larkspur, lemon tree, lettuce, licorice, lilac, lily, lobelia, lotus, lucky hand root, maidenhair fern, mallows, mimosa, moonwort, morning glory, myrrh, myrtle tree, orchid, orris, pansy, papaya, passionflower, peach tree, pear tree, periwinkle, persimmon, plum tree, poplar tree, poppies, purslane, ragwort, raspberry, rose, sandalwood, scullcap, skunk cabbage, Solomon's seal, spearmint, spikenard, strawberry, sugar cane, sweetpea, tamarind, tamarisk, tansy, thyme, tomato, tonka beans, trillium, valerian, vanilla, violet, willow tree, wintergreen, wolfsbane, yarrow, and yew.

9

Green Healing

The following herbs are used in Wiccan spells and rituals to promote the general healing of the body, mind, and spirit: adder's tongue, allspice, amaranth, angelica, apple, balm of Gilead, barley, bay tree, bittersweet, blackberry, bracken, burdock, calamus, carnation, cedar, cinnamon, citron, cowslip, cucumber, dock, elder, eucalyptus, fennel, figwort, flax, gardenia, garlic, ginseng, goat's rue, goldenseal, groundsel, heliotrope, hemp, henna, hops, horehound, horse chestnut, ivy, Job's tears, lemon balm, life everlasting, lime, mesquite, mints, mugwort, myrrh, nettle, oak tree, olive leaves, onion, peppermint, pepper tree, persimmon, pine trees, plantain, rose, rosemary, rowan tree, rue, saffron, sandalwood, spearmint, thistle, thyme, Ti plant, tobacco (used mostly by Native American healers and shamans), vervain, violet, wild plum, willow tree, wintergreen, wood sorrel, and yerba santa.

To attain longevity, the following herbs are magickally used: cypress, lavender, lemon, life everlasting, maple tree, peach tree, sage, and tansy.

The following herbal oils are used magickally by Wiccans and modern Witches to promote the general healing of the body, mind, and spirit. They can be rubbed on the body as a massage oil, added to homemade healing candles, or used to anoint healing poppets: carnation, eucalyptus, gardenia, lotus, myrrh, narcissus, rosemary, sandalwood, and violet.

For vitality, the following healing oils are magickally used: allspice, carnation, rosemary, and vanilla.

Birth Herbs

Lavender is an herb of purification and protection, and one of the primary magickal herbs used by Green Witch midwives for the sacred rite of childbirth.

A handful of lavender flowers infused in one pint of sweet almond or apricot kernel oil can be used for gently massaging the mother-to-be as she focuses on relaxing to the rhythms of her labor.

Hang lavender sprigs over the door of the delivery room to banish and protect against any negative or malevolent energies.

To ease tension and fear during labor, take a warm herbal bath by candlelight (as long as the baby's water bag remains unbroken). Lavender combined with comfrey, rosemary, sage, and sea salt makes an excellent herbal bath which is both soothing to the spirit and antiseptic. (Add one cup of the herbs and one-fourth cup of sea salt to two quarts of water. Heat almost to a boil. Immediately remove from heat; cover and steep for one hour. Strain before adding to your bathwater.)

If sipped during labor, a tea made from red raspberry leaves will help to relieve the feeling of nausea, which is commonly experienced by women prior to and during the birthing process.

To help ease the pains of childbirth, wear a birthing charm bag containing quartz crystals (or a bloodstone) and any of the following magickal birth herbs: alfalfa, angelica, Bethroot, birthroot, comfrey, elder flowers, lavender, lemon balm, mints, motherwort, nettles, raspberry leaves, sage, or squawvine.

Both the leaves and seeds of dill have long been used by herbalists in both the United States and Europe as a milk stimulant for nursing mothers. Dill also relieves congestion in the breast due to breastfeeding.

To prepare an infusion, steep two teaspoons of dill seeds in one cup of water for about fifteen minutes. Drink half a cup four times daily. Another method which is just as effective is to add eight drops of dill oil to one pint of water. Take one teaspoonful up to eight times a day.

In addition to drinking "dill water," you can also wear a consecrated charm bag filled with dillweed between your breasts.

Herbs to Avoid During Pregnancy

Despite the fact that some herb books refer to blue cohosh as a "woman's herb" and suggest that it be used to stimulate the uterus or hasten childbirth, blue cohosh is an unsafe plant for self-medication and should never be used by pregnant women. This herb contains an organic compound which has a toxic effect on the cardiac muscle.

It can also produce high blood pressure and do severe harm to the intestines.

The following herbs are classified as abortifacients, which means they can induce an abortion: angelica, juniper, may apple, pennyroyal, rue, and tansy.

Other herbs that should be avoided by women during pregnancy include catnip (which may greatly increase menstrual flow), licorice (which may cause edema in pregnant women), gentian (which can cause nausea and vomiting to occur), marjoram (which can cause uterine irritation to develop if used during pregnancy or menstruation), and parsley oil or large quantities of parsley (which can have a toxic effect).

Healing Herb Baths

One of the best ways to prepare an herbal bath is to wrap a handful of the appropriate herb (or herbs) in a piece of cheesecloth and hang it from the bathtub faucet while the water runs to fill your bath. After the tub is full, turn off the water and steep the bundle in the hot bathwater for about ten minutes. Remove it (be sure to squeeze out all of the herb water from it) and then enjoy your bath.

Another popular method is to place your bath herbs in a large tea infuser with a chain and then hang it beneath the faucet as you fill the tub with hot water.

Or, if you prefer, you can prepare an herbal bath by making a strong infusion from your herbs and adding it to your bathwater. To do this, place half a cup of the appropriate herb (or herbs) in a cauldron or other container. Cover with one quart of boiling water. Allow it to steep for about twenty minutes and then strain out the liquid into your bathwater.

For a tonic bath, use any combination of the following herbs: blackberry leaves, comfrey, daisy, dandelion, ginseng root, jasmine flowers, lavender, nettle, orange blossoms, patchouli, raspberry leaves, and rose petals.

To relieve tension and soothe the nerves, soak your body in a warm herbal bath in which any of the following herbs have been added: catnip, chamomile flowers, comfrey, elder, evening primrose flowers, hyssop, jasmine flowers, juniper berries, lemon balm, linden flowers, marsh mallow roots, melilot, mullein, passionflower, rose petals, slippery elm (inner bark), tansy flowers, valerian roots, vervain, and violet.

To make your herbal bath even more relaxing, bathe by the light of blue or white candles while listening to your favorite relaxing music.

Any combination of the following healing herbs are ideal for baths to relieve muscular aches or stiffness of the joints: agrimony, bay, juniper berries, mugwort, oregano, poplar (bark and buds), sage, and strawberry leaves.

To aid circulation, prepare an herbal bath using equal parts of bladder wrack, marigold, and nettle. To promote circulation in the treatment of arthritis, bursitis, or gout, traditional healers of the Orient boil two pounds of grated ginger in one gallon of water for about ten minutes. The mixture is then strained through a cheesecloth to remove the ginger, and the herbal water is then added to the warm bathwater.

To induce sweating, add burdock root or hyssop to the bathwater. Both of these herbs possess diaphoretic properties.

To soothe varicose veins or heal body scars, soak daily in an herbal bath prepared with the leaves of the marigold.

A hot bath in which eucalyptus has been added will help ease a cold or the flu and will aid in clearing congestion of both the lungs and the nasal passages. Eucalyptus also contains antiseptic properties.

To relieve minor skin inflammations, soak in a cool or lukewarm bath prepared with any of the following herbs:

alder, dandelion leaves, elecampane, lady's mantle, mint, or plantain.

The following bath herbs are classified as astringents, which means that they constrict the tissues and are used to stop bleeding, close skin pores, and tighten up loose muscles: agrimony, alum root, bay, bayberry (bark), clary, comfrey (leaves and root), dock, frankincense resin, lady's mantle, lemongrass, mullein, myrrh resin, nasturtium flowers, periwinkle, potentilla root, queen of the meadow, raspberry leaves, rose petals, rosemary, strawberry, white willow bark, wintergreen, Witch hazel (bark and leaves), yarrow flowers.

The following bath herbs are classified as stimulants, which means that they increase or accelerate the various functional actions of the organs and rapidly stimulate general health: basil, bay, calendula flowers, citronella, fennel, horseradish roots, lavender flowers, lemon verbena, lovage roots, marjoram, mint, nettle, pine (needles), queen of the meadow, rosemary, sage, savory, thyme, and vetivert roots.

If your feet are tired and sore, pamper them by soaking them in a warm and soothing footbath prepared with any combination of the following herbs: agrimony, alder bark, burdock, goat's rue, lavender flowers, mustard seed, sage, Witch hazel (bark and leaves), and wormwood.

If your health has been weakened by sorcery, psychic attack, or malevolent supernatural entities of any kind, a bath prepared with any combination of the following herbs will rejuvenate your body and spirit, as well as offer you magickal protection: agrimony, angelica root, bay, cloves, elder, eucalyptus, geranium, hyssop, juniper berries, marjoram, mint, mugwort, myrrh resin, pine (needles), raspberry leaves, rose petals, sage, valerian root, and vervain.

Traditional Chinese Medicine

For centuries, Taoists and Shaolin Buddhist monks have used various herbs not only to improve health, prevent disease, and balance the mind and body, but as part of their spiritual path as well. They found that the use of certain herbs could help develop consciousness and enhance both their meditations and martial arts practices.

In the traditional Chinese healing arts and in the theory of the Tao, the "Three Treasures" play an important role: They are Qi (the life force), Jing (essence), and Shen (the driving force behind Qi and Jing). They must be nourished daily with herbs and meditation in order for one to attain health, long life, and spiritual enlightenment.

Many of the tonic herbs used by Taoists can be purchased in the United States in herb shops, health food stores, and even Chinese grocery stores (which can be found in any metropolitan Chinatown district).

Ginseng, a mystical root shaped like a human figure, is considered to be the ultimate aphrodisiac by many folks around the world and is one Chinese tonic herb nearly everyone is familiar with.

It is believed that ginseng has been used by people in the northern regions of China since prehistoric times.

As an herb of healing, ginseng has been documented as being beneficial in treating specific diseases such as anemia, atherosclerosis, depression, diabetes, edema, hypertension, and ulcers. According to folk traditions, there are over seventy medical ailments which can be successfully treated with ginseng.

Korean red ginseng (the most popular type of ginseng sold in the United States) tonifies the Qi and nourishes the Shen. It also is a beneficial stimulant for those who suffer from fatigue or emotional burnout.

The best preparation of ginseng to use is any liquid tonic that has the root in the bottle with it.

Xi Yang Shen (North American ginseng; a very different but close relative to Korean red ginseng) calms the mind, balances the yin energies, and nourishes the Shen.

Dang Shen (another type of ginseng which is usually less expensive than the others) nourishes the Qi and is a beneficial tonic for persons whose energy levels are feeling low.

The root known as Dang Gui calms the mind, regulates the menses, and restores energy. Although it is valued as a beneficial blood tonic by persons of both sexes, Dang Gui is known as "the woman's herb."

Hong Zao (red fruit date) nourishes the Qi and is known for its harmonizing action. It helps build physical strength, calms the mind, and moistens and purifies the viscera.

Gan Cao (Chinese licorice) also nourishes the Qi and is used by Taoists to energize and detoxify the body and to enhance the powers of concentration.

Wu Wei Zi (five-flavored fruit) is associated with the five ancient Chinese elements of Fire, Water, Wood, Metal, and Earth and is highly valued as a longevity herb and a female sexual tonic. To make a traditional tea, boil six grams of Wu Wei Zi berries in three cups of water for a half an hour.

A very popular and relatively inexpensive Chinese herb is the He Shou Wu, which is sold in many health food stores in pill form and under the name of Shou Wu Pian. This herb nourishes the Jing and calms the mind. It is also valued as an herb of longevity.

Gou Qi Zi (Chinese wolfberry) is also reputed to be an herb of longevity. The berries (which are often used in Chinese cooking recipes in place of raisins) are valued as a yin tonic and are said to have a calming effect on the liver. They tonify the blood and brighten the eyes.

Wolfberry tea can easily be made by boiling a handful of the berries in three cups of water for a half an hour.

Herbal remedies are a mainstay of traditional Chinese medicine, and the oldest known herb book is the Chinese *Pen-ts'ao* ("Herbal") written by the Emperor Shen-nung. Recorded in this book are over three hundred medicinal herb preparations.

10

Dangerous Plants

Herbs can bring magick, healing and happiness into one's life; however, certain plants can be very dangerous or even deadly if taken internally or used in an incorrect manner. Therefore, it cannot be stressed strongly enough that extreme caution should always be observed when handling unfamiliar plants or using them to season food or in home remedies or magickal potions intended for human consumption.

There are some plants (poinsettia leaves, for example)

that are extremely poisonous to animals. There are also many plants that animals and birds can safely eat but are highly toxic to humans.

Many herbs regarded as non-poisonous (such as marjoram and parsley) have found their way into this chapter because they can cause harm to pregnant women or be potentially dangerous if taken in large quantities (such as licorice).

The plants found in this chapter are not intended to represent a complete list of every dangerous plant in the world. Therefore, if a particular plant does not appear on the following list, that does not necessarily mean that it is not poisonous or capable of producing unpleasant side-effects if ingested or used medicinally without proper medical supervision.

By the same token, not every plant listed in this chapter will kill you or make you sick if used correctly or in moderate doses, and so forth.

The main thing is for you to be well-informed and always use wise judgement. Do not attempt to use herbs with medicinal properties for self-medication. Even plants that are generally safe can still bring on severe allergic reactions among certain individuals. Another important thing to always bear in mind is that a recommended dose of a healing herb considered safe for an adult may not be so safe for a child.

In case of any medical emergency, please contact a qualified physician or a paramedic immediately, or seek proper treatment at a hospital.

Aconite (*Aconitum napellus*): Also known by the names "wolfbane" and "monkshood," aconite is an extremely dangerous plant containing a number of highly toxic alkaloids. It is classified as a perennial and has violet-blue hood-shaped flowers (hence its nickname "monkshood"). It is a beautiful plant which many gardeners use as an ornamental; however, extreme caution should be exercised and gloves should be worn whenever handling aconite, for its poison (aconitine) can easily be absorbed into the system through the skin.

Aloe Vera (genus *Aloe*): The aloe vera plant has been used for centuries as a natural home remedy to heal burns, minor cuts, poison ivy, and skin cancer. It is perfectly safe and effective when used externally; however, it can produce severe intestinal pain and violent purgation if swallowed.

American Hellebore (genus *Helleborus*): If taken internally, this plant can cause a number of unpleasant reactions ranging from diarrhea, nausea, and abdominal pain to impaired vision, unconsciousness, and paralysis. Sometimes ingestion of American hellebore can lead to death.

American Mandrake : *See* Mayapple

Arnica (genus *Arnica*): Never take arnica internally, for it greatly increases the blood pressure and has a toxic action on the heart. While generally considered safe when used externally (usually in liniments and salves to relieve pain and reduce inflammations), the helenalin in arnica can cause sensitive individuals to develop dermatitis.

Autumn Crocus (*Colchium autumnale*): Used by the ancient Romans and Greeks as a powerful herbal medicine to treat gout, the autumn crocus is an extremely poisonous plant and should never be eaten. All parts of the plant are toxic and can cause the user to experience diarrhea, nausea, severe pain in the intestines, and kidney damage. An overdose of colchicine (a highly poisonous alkaloid which is extracted from the corm and seeds of the plant) may cause death.

Baneberry: Baneberry is the name given to any plant of

the genus *Actaea*. Often called "cohosh," this plant has red or white berries which are extremely poisonous and should never be eaten.

Belladonna: *See* Deadly Nightshade

Bitterroot: *See* Gentian

Bittersweet (*Solanum dulcamara*): The scarlet-colored berries of this sprawling vine are poisonous to humans if eaten. The bittersweet is a native to Europe and Asia and is sometimes referred to as "nightshade."

Bitterwort: See Gentian

Black Bryony (*Tamus communis*): The red berries of this climbing European plant are very poisonous to humans if eaten.

Black Hellebore (genus *Helleborus*): This is a very poisonous plant, and under no circumstances should any part of it ever be ingested. Take care to wear gloves when handling it in the garden, for its leaves when bruised have been known to cause severe dermatitis in some people.

Black Horehound (*Ballota nigra*): Not to be confused with the horehound of cough syrup fame (*Marrubiam vulgare*), the black horehound is a foul-smelling weed which is extremely poisonous to humans if large enough quantities are ingested.

Black Nightshade: *See* Deadly Nightshade

Bloodroot (*Sanguinaria canadensis*): This plant possesses many wonderful healing properties and is generally considered not to be poisonous; however, it should not be used medicinally without proper medical supervision.

Ingesting this herb may cause headaches, nausea, vomiting, and tunnel vision to occur in some individuals. A toxic dose may result in paralysis, vertigo, and temporary blindness.

Blue Cohosh (*Caulophyllum thalictroides*): Do not take this herb internally, especially if you suffer from high blood pressure. Blue cohosh contains the glycoside caulosaponin, which constricts the blood vessels of the heart, damages the intestines, and irritates the mucous membranes. The blue seeds of this plant have been known to poison children to death.

Broom (genus *Cytisus*): Do not eat the flowering stem tops of the broom (especially before blooming), for they contain a substance called sparteine which causes diarrhea, vertigo, headache, and nausea, among other things. Large doses of Scotch broom can be deadly.

Bull's Foot: *See* Coltsfoot

Burning Bush: *See* Wahoo

Calabar Bean: Also known as "ordeal bean," the calabar bean is a dark brown seed from an African vine, *Physostigma venenosum*. It is the source of the drug physostigmine and can have a poisonous effect on humans if taken internally without the proper supervision of a medical expert.

Calico Bush: *See* Mountain Laurel

Castor Bean: *See* Castor-Oil Plant

Castor-Oil Plant (*Ricinus communis*): Do not eat the seeds of the castor-oil plant (or castor bean), because they are poisonous and can cause severe illness and death.

(One seed alone can be fatal to a small child!) The leaves can cause a skin rash in sensitive individuals if touched. The oil from this plant (which is extracted commercially and often prescribed as a laxative) is fairly mild; however, excessive amounts can cause blurred vision, diarrhea, and vomiting.

Cat's Tail: *See* Horsetail

Cayenne Pepper Plant (*Capsicum frutescens*): Cayenne pepper is widely used as a condiment and as a folk remedy for various ailments. Cayenne pepper is not poisonous; however, kidney damage can result from ingesting large amounts of it over a period of time. It can also be dangerous to the health of individuals who suffer from chronic bowel diseases, duodenal ulcers, and other intestinal disorders.

Celandine (*Chelidonium majus*): Celandine contains an opium alkaloid, and all parts of the plant are used medicinally. It should not be used in herbal home remedies without proper medical supervision.

Christmas Rose: *See Black Hellebore*

Colchium: *See* Autumn Crocus

Coltsfoot (*Tussilago farfara*): In the mid-1970s, a study conducted by Japanese scientists found the flowers and leaves of the coltsfoot to be cancer-causing to the liver when taken internally, and they concluded that the plant was therefore unsafe for medicinal purposes.

Columbine (genus *Aquilegia*): Columbine is used as a medicinal herb both internally and externally; however, it contains prussic acid and narcotic properties and should only be used under proper medical supervision.

Coughwort: *See* Coltsfoot

Cowbane (*Oxypolis rigidior*): The cowbane is a white-flowered plant which grows wild in the southeastern and central parts of the United States. It is related to the water hemlock and has extremely poisonous roots and foliage.

Crystalwort: *See* Liverleaf

Deadly Nightshade (*Solanum nigrum*): A wicked component of hellbroths and flying ointments of the Middle Ages, the deadly nightshade is a purple-flowered plant that everyone (including modern Witches) should avoid. Its berries are extremely toxic, producing hallucinations, paralysis, coma, and often death if eaten. Even touching the plant can be potentially dangerous as its poisonous chemicals are absorbed into the system through the skin.

Devil's Apple: *See* Mayapple

Dog's Mercury (*Mercurialis perennis*): The seeds of this creeping, foul-smelling Old World weed are poisonous to humans if taken internally.

Duck's Foot: *See* Mayapple

Dwale: *See* Deadly Nightshade

Elderberry (genus *Sambucus*): Do not experiment medicinally with the leaves, stems, or roots of elderberry shrubs, because they contain cyanide-releasing substances which can cause severe illness. However, the flowers and berries (when ripe and cooked) are considered to be harmless.

Ergot (*Clavicops purpurea*): This is a poisonous fungus that infects various cereal plants, especially rye. It is medicinally potent and should not be used in any herbal home remedy. The hallucinogenic chemical LSD (lysergic acid diethylamide) is a synthetic derivative of ergot.

Eucalyptus (genus *Eucalyptus*): Large doses of eucalyptus oil (called "eucalyptol") can result in unpleasant reactions such as diarrhea, muscle spasms, nausea, and vomiting. Never apply eucalyptus oil directly on the skin unless it has been properly diluted with alcohol, oil, or water, and take care to avoid getting it in or near the eyes.

Eyebright (*Euphrasia officinalis*): Eyebright has been used by herbalists and folk healers as an eye medication since ancient times; however, modern scientific studies have been unable to establish its effectiveness in the treatment of eye disease. The use of homemade eyebright tinctures can result in various eye ailments, flulike symptoms, constipation, insomnia, and aching teeth.

Fall Dandelion: *See* Arnica

Flax (*Linum usitatissimum*): The immature seed pods of the flax (or linseed) are poisonous and, if ingested, can produce symptoms such as convulsions, weakness, increased respiratory rate, shortness of breath, nervousness, staggering, and paralysis.

Fly Agaric: *See* chapter 5: "Mind-Altering Plants"

Foal's Foot: *See* Coltsfoot

Foxglove (*Digitalis purpurea*): Foxglove, the source of the powerful heart stimulant digitalis, is an important medicinal plant. However, all parts of the plant are extremely poisonous if ingested, often causing severe illness followed by death. Under no circumstances should you ever experiment medicinally with foxglove.

Gentian (*Gentiana lutea*): Do not use gentian root internally if you suffer from high blood pressure or are pregnant. An overdose of gentian root (usually anything more than thirty grams) can result in nausea and vomiting.

Goldenseal (*Hydrastis canadensis*): Goldenseal should not be taken internally. Hydrastine, which is its major component, is dangerous and can produce such toxic reactions as convulsions, respiratory failure, diarrhea, vomiting, miscarriage, and even fatal paralysis. An external overdose of goldenseal can result in severe skin ulceration, and under no circumstances should it ever be used as a douche.

Ground Lemon: *See* Mayapple

Hellebore: *See* American Hellebore and Black Hellebore

Hemlock: *See* Poison Hemlock

Henbane (*Hyoscyamus niger*): A native to the Mediterranean region, this highly toxic plant was infamous in the Middle Ages as an herb of the Black Arts and a main ingredient in the poisonous hellbroths of evil sorceresses. It should never be used in any herbal home remedies. Ingestion can cause severe sickness, frightening hallucinations, coma, and death.

Hepatica: *See* Liverleaf

Hog Apple: *See* Mayapple

Holly: *See* Ilex

Honeysuckle (genus *Lonicera*): The vines and fruit of

this fragrant flowering plant are extremely poisonous to humans if taken internally. Do not use them in any herbal home remedies or magickal potions which are intended for drinking.

Horse Balm (*Collinsonia canadensis*): A native of the eastern parts of the United States and Canada, the horse balm with its lemon-scented flowers is very poisonous if eaten. Be sure to keep children and pets away from it.

Horse Hoof: *See* Coltsfoot

Horse Foot: *See* Coltsfoot

Horsetail (genus *Equisetum*): Large doses of horsetail herb are toxic. Horsetails which grow in highly fertilized soil are especially poisonous if ingested, for they are known to absorb the nitrates and selenium from the ground.

Ilex (genus *Ilex*): Also known as holly, this plant (which is a traditional Yuletide decoration) possesses poisonous seeds and berries which should never be eaten or used in herbal home remedies.

Impatiens (genus *Impatiens*): The impatiens (also known as jewelweed) is a beautiful flowering plant found in many gardens. It is lovely to look at but very poisonous if eaten. Its ripe pods burst open when touched.

Indigo (genus *Indigofera*): It is wise not to use indigo in any herbal home remedies, because many species of this plant are highly toxic and none of indigo's reputed cures have ever been scientifically proven.

Indian Apple: *See* Mayapple

Indian Tobacco: *See* Lobelia

Indian Turnip: *See* Jack-in-the-Pulpit

Inkberry: *See* Pokeweed

Jack-in-the-Pulpit (*Arisaema triphyllum*): This spring-flowering woodland herb is a native of the eastern parts of the United States and Canada. It has a root which is very poisonous to humans, and it should never be eaten or used in any herbal home remedies.

Jerusalem Cherry (*Solanum pseudo-capsicum*): Often used as a houseplant, this Old World plant bears a reddish fruit that is extremely poisonous if eaten.

Jewelweed: *See* Impatiens

Jimsonweed: *See* chapter 5: "Mind-Altering Plants"

Juniper (genus *Juniperus*): Do not use juniper internally as a folk medicine if you suffer from kidney ailments or are pregnant. Convulsions, personality changes, and severe damage to the kidneys may result from small, repeated doses. An overdose may cause elevated blood pressure, accelerated heartbeat, convulsions, miscarriage, and intense pain in or near the kidneys.

Laurel: *See* Mountain Laurel

Leopard's Bane: *See* Arnica

Lettuce Opium: *See* Prickly Lettuce

Licorice (*Glycyrrhiza glabra*): Licorice should not be used by cardiac patients, pregnant women, or anyone who suffers from kidney ailments, hypertension, or obesity. Large doses of licorice over extended periods of time can be extremely poisonous to the system.

Lily of the Valley (*Convallaria majalis*): The lily of the valley should never be ingested or used as a medicinal herb in any home remedies. It is toxic and contains the poisons convallarin and convallamarin, which may raise the blood pressure to dangerous levels and interfere with the normal function of the heart, lungs, and other organs.

Liverleaf (*Hepatica americana*): Used medicinally as an astringent and powerful remedy for ailments of the liver and gallbladder, the liverleaf plant (before being dried) contains an extremely irritating poison which first stimulates and then paralyzes the central nervous system.

Liverwort: *See* Liverleaf

Lobelia (genus *Lobelia*): All parts of this plant are poisonous and may kill you if you take them internally! Do not use lobelia in any herbal folk remedies. Even a small amount of the dried herb (as little as fifty milligrams) can cause uncontrollable vomiting, coma, convulsions, paralysis, and death.

Mandrake (*Mandragora officinarum*): The European mandrake with its human-shaped root is by far the most magickal of plants and certainly one of the deadliest! It is a highly poisonous narcotic with properties similar to those of deadly nightshade (belladonna). Internal use of mandrake may cause you to experience frightening hallucinations, convulsions, heart damage, coma, or quite possibly death. Use it wisely in the art of spellcraft, but under no circumstances should you ever eat it, use it in any herbal remedies, or add it to any potions which are intended for human consumption.

Marjoram (*Marjorana hortensis*): Marjoram is a safe culinary and medicinal herb; however, it should not be used by women who are pregnant or menstruating because it can cause severe irritation of the uterus.

Mayapple (*Podophyllum peltatum*): Also known as "American mandrake" (among other names), the mayapple is a deadly plant which should be handled only with extreme caution or avoided completely. All parts of it are poisonous, except for its fruit, which ripens in September. (But be careful not to eat its seeds, for they are poisonous also!) An overdose can result in death, and even touching the plant can have deadly consequences, as the poison is absorbed into the skin.

Mayflower: *See* Trailing Arbutus

Meadow Crocus: *See* Autumn Crocus

Meadow Saffron: *See* Autumn Crocus

Milkweed (genus *Astragalus*): A fragrant native plant of eastern North America with milky juice (hence its name), the milkweed is poisonous to humans if taken internally.

Mistletoe (*Viscum album*): Kissing under the mistletoe and using it to decorate a Yuletide altar are wonderful old traditions; however, the berries and leaves of this Eurasian parasitic shrub are highly poisonous and should never be eaten or used in any homemade herbal remedies. They are known to cause hallucinations, heart attacks, convulsions, elevated blood pressure, and even death.

Monkshood: *See* Aconite

Mountain Arnica: *See* Arnica

Mountain Laurel (*Kalmia latifolia*): This evergreen shrub is a native of the eastern parts of the United States and Canada. It has clusters of pink or white flowers and leaves that are very poisonous to humans if taken internally.

Mountain Tobacco: *See* Arnica

Nux Vomica (*Strychnos nux-vomica*): Do not eat the seeds of this Asian tree. They are very deadly and are the source of strychnine (a poison used for killing rats), brucine, and the medical preparation nux vomica (which induces vomiting).

Oleander (*Nerium oleander*): The oleander is a flowering shrub that grows mainly in warm climates. Its leaves and flowers must never be eaten, for they are quite poisonous. Oleander sometimes causes skin rashes if handled without gloves.

Opium Poppy: *See* chapter 5: "Mind Altering Plants"

Ordeal Bean: *See* Calabar Bean

Paddock Pipes: *See* Horsetail

Papoose Root: *See* Blue Cohosh

Parsley (*Petroselinum crispum*): It is advisable not to use parsley oil or ingest large quantities of the herb if you are a pregnant woman. Large doses of extracted parsley camphor (one of the volatile oils of the plant which gives it its distinctive aroma) can be toxic, causing a decrease in pulse rate and blood pressure, followed by muscle weakness and paralysis. Congestion of the lungs and swelling of the liver are also possible.

Pennyroyal (*Mentha pulegium*): Since early times, pennyroyal has been used to induce menstruation or to cause abortion; however, the oil in its leaves contains a toxic chemical that can cause severe liver damage, convulsions, coma, and death. The oil from both the American and European pennyroyal plants should be avoided. Pennyroyal tea is considered by most herbalists to be nontoxic, since it does not contain enough of the oil to be harmful. Pennyroyal tea is sometimes used as an herbal remedy to aid digestion and soothe an upset stomach; however, peppermint tea is more effective and safe to use.

Pewter Grass: *See* Horsetail

Poinsettia (*Euphorbia pulcherrima*): This tropical American shrub is a Yuletide favorite; however, its leaves are very toxic to both humans and animals if eaten. Be sure to keep poinsettia plants out of the reach of small children and pets to avoid accidental poisonings.

Poison Dogwood: *See* Poison Sumac

Poison Elder: *See* Poison Sumac

Poison Hemlock (*Conium maculatum*): As its name implies, the poison hemlock is an extremely poisonous plant and should never be eaten or experimented with in any way. Hemlock was the poison of choice for Socrates, who took his own life after being condemned to die.

Poison Ivy (*Rhus radicans*): Anyone who's ever been exposed to poison ivy by accident knows how uncomfortable the rash, itching, and blisters it produces can be. In addition to allergic contact dermatitis, some individuals suffer more serious reactions such as headache, generalized swelling, fever, and malaise. Poison ivy is usually simply treated with calamine or other soothing ointments; however, a physician should be immediately consulted if a person exposed to poison ivy develops a high fever, a widespread rash, or a rash involving the eyes, mouth, or genital area.

Poison Lettuce: *See* Prickly Lettuce

Poison Oak (*Rhus toxicodendron* or *Rhus diversiloba*): Both shrubs are related to poison ivy and can cause similar reactions. *For more information, see* Poison Ivy.

Poison Root: *See* Poison Hemlock

Poison Snakewood: *See* Poison Hemlock

Poison Sumac (*Rhus vernix*): The poison sumac is a swamp shrub which grows mainly in the southeastern United States. It is related to poison ivy and causes similar reactions. *For more information, see* Poison Ivy.

Poke: *See* Pokeweed

Pokeberry: *See* Pokeweed

Poke Root: *See* Pokeweed

Pokeweed (*Phytolacca americana*): The pokeweed is extremely poisonous, especially its root, berries, and seeds. It should never be eaten, and gloves should always be worn whenever handling this plant. Pokeweed possesses narcotic properties, and overdoses can sometimes result in death.

Prickly Lettuce (*Lactuca scariola*): The young leaves of this plant are sometimes used in salads and as a potherb; however, the prickly lettuce is classified as narcotic (nonaddictive) and poisonous. Also known by the nickname "wild opium," its milky juice (lactucarium) was used in the eighteenth and early nineteenth centuries as a substitute for opium.

Psilocybe Mushroom: *See* chapter 5: "Mind-Altering Plants"

Racoon Berry: *See* Mayapple

Rhubarb (*Rheum rhaponticum*): The raw stalklike leaves of the rhubarb plant are poisonous if eaten. They are edible only after being sweetened and cooked. The roots and rhizome of the Asian variety (*Rheum officinale* or *Rheum palmatum*) have a laxative effect when ingested and should be used only under the supervision of a trained medical professional.

Rosebay: *See* Oleander

Rue (*Ruta graveolens*): Used in the Middle Ages as an antisorcery herb, rue is a poisonous plant which should be avoided. Although it rarely causes death, rue can cause convulsions, vomiting, prostration, and severe pain in the stomach and intestines if taken internally in large doses. Rue contains a dangerous oil which is capable of inducing abortion; therefore, it should never be used by pregnant women. Gloves should always be worn when handling rue, because the leaves, flowers, and fruit often cause itchy and burning skin rashes.

Saffron (*Crocus sativus*): Saffron has been used safely as both a medicinal herb and a culinary spice since the fourteenth century; however, a dose of one-third of an ounce or more taken internally can be toxic to the system.

Saint John's Wort (*Hypericum perforatum*): Many centuries ago, Saint John's Wort was burned by superstitious peasants and royalty alike to dispel evil spirits, drive away devils, and protect against sorcery. It should never be taken internally by persons who are fair-skinned, because it may cause photosensitivity, resulting in skin rashes, inflamed membranes, and other toxic reactions.

Sassafras (*Sassafras albidum*): Its roots were once used as a flavoring agent in root beer; however, sassafras (along with sassafras oil and safrole—a chemical constituent of sassafras) has since been outlawed by the Food and Drug Administration from use in foods after scientific research in the 1960s determined it to be a toxic carcinogen. A dose of the volatile oil as small as one teaspoon results in degeneration of the heart, liver, and kidneys. However, external use of the plant is considered to be perfectly safe.

Shave Grass: *See* Horsetail

Snow-on-the-Mountain (*Euphorbia marginata*): A native to central North America, the snow-on-the-mountain is very poisonous to humans if taken internally.

Spotted Hemlock: *See* Poison Hemlock

Spurge (genus *Euphorbia*): Spurge has a strong purgative effect when taken internally. An overdose may cause diarrhea, abdominal cramps, nausea, vomiting, and other toxic reactions. Spurge should not be used without proper medical supervision.

Stinking Horehound: *See* Black Horehound

Stramonium: *See* Jimsonweed

Swallow Wort: *See* Celandine

Sweet Flag (*Acorus calamus*): Sweet flag has long been used as a medicinal herb and a culinary spice; however, recent scientific studies have found that the plant contains an oil which is carcinogenic. Although it is still available at most supermarkets, its use is not recommended.

Tansy (*Tanacetum vulgare*): As a culinary herb, tansy

should be used in moderation, because large amounts of it are potentially toxic, causing violent reactions and death. The oil from the tansy is also quite poisonous, and as little as ten drops can cause death.

Thorn Apple: *See* Jimsonweed

Tobacco (*Nicotiana tabacum*): Tobacco is a plant native to tropical North America; it's leaves are used primarily for making cigarettes, cigars, snuff, pipe tobacco, and chewing tobacco. Tobacco contains an addictive and poisonous alkaloid called nicotine (which is used as an insecticide). The smoking of tobacco products is the primary cause of lung cancer, pulmonary diseases and cancers of the mouth, larnyx, throat, esophagus, bladder, kidneys, and pancreas. The carcinogenic tar in tobacco smoke can inflame and clog airways of the lungs, leading to bronchitis and emphysema. Smoking is also a major risk factor contributing to heart attack. Pregnant women should refrain from smoking tobacco, as it increases the risk of spontaneous abortion and stillbirth. Since addiction to nicotine is difficult to break, the best advice is not to smoke in the first place. Chewing tobacco is also a health risk, as it is the main cause of oral cancers.

Trailing Arbutus (*Epigaea repens*): The trailing arbutus, which grows primarily in the eastern regions of North America, is very poisonous to humans if taken internally.

Tropical Periwinkle (*Vinca*): Do not use tropical periwinkle medicinally without proper medical supervision. This is an extremely potent plant, and an overdose can result in lethal poisoning. Large doses may produce convulsions, damage to the liver and nervous system, psychosis, hallucinations, and coma. Suppression of the immune system and impaired bone marrow function are also possible.

Valerian (*Valeriana officinalis*): Valerian is considered by most herbalists to be safe and effective; however, excessive amounts taken internally may cause the user to experience dizzy spells, stupor, and vomiting. Prolonged use of this herb should be avoided, for it may cause severe depression over a period of time.

Vervain (*Verbena officinalis*): Vervain (a sacred plant to the ancients and a popular medicinal herb in medieval times) has been reputed for centuries to be a powerful healer of various ailments and diseases; however, its astonishing healing powers have yet to be scientifically proven. Do not take vervain internally, because even a moderate amount of the herb will cause vomiting.

Violet (genus *Viola*): The violet is not a toxic plant; however, it is wise not to ingest its seeds, for they may cause you to experience stomach discomfort and vomiting.

Virginia Snakeroot (*Aristolochia serpentaria*): Do not attempt to use Virginia snakeroot medicinally, for an internal overdose may result in vomiting, dizziness, intense pain in the bowels, and death by respiratory paralysis.

Wahoo (*Euonymus atropurpureus*): The bark, leaves, and berries of the wahoo possess dangerous emetic and purgative properties. Children can be fatally poisoned by consuming as little as three of its brightly-colored berries. Adults may experience vomiting, diarrhea, and convulsions for about twelve hours, followed by unconsciousness.

Water Hemlock: *See* Poison Hemlock

White Bryony (*Bryonia dioica*): The berries of this climbing European vine are extremely poisonous to humans and should never be eaten or used in any herbal home remedies.

White Snakeroot (*Eupatorium rugosum*): The white snakeroot, a native North American plant with heart-shaped leaves and clusters of tiny white flowers, is extremely poisonous to humans if taken internally. Never eat or use white snakeroot in any herbal home remedies.

Wild Lettuce: *See* chapter 5: "Mind-Altering Plants"

Wild Saffron: *See* Autumn Crocus

Winter Rose: *See* Black Hellebore

Woad (*Isatis tinctoria*): Do not use this herb internally, for it is extremely poisonous. It should never be used in any herbal home remedies or magickal potions which are intended for drinking.

Wolfsbane: *See* Aconite

Wood Anemone (*Anemone quinquefolia*): Do not eat the seeds of this white-flowered plant, for they are extremely poisonous to humans.

Wormwood (*Artemesia absinthium*): Once used as an ingredient in absinthe, wormwood contains an essential oil which is an active narcotic poison. Large doses or prolonged use of wormwood may cause the user to experience vertigo, insomnia, nervousness, convulsions, nightmares, and vomiting.

Yew (genus *Taxus*): The yew is an evergreen tree or shrub with scarlet-colored berries and seeds that are extremely poisonous to humans if taken internally.

Yohimbe: *See* chapter 5: "Mind-Altering Plants"

11

Herb Omens and
Superstitions

Superstitious beliefs have been connected with flowers and trees since the earliest of times. The exact origins of most of these folk legends and old wives' tales are unknown, but they appear in every culture throughout the world and reflect the curious customs, religious practices, and beliefs of the past.

Superstitions (which, interestingly, were not regarded as

such until the middle part of the nineteenth century) were at one time considered to be "products of heathenism" as the Pagan religions of pre-Christian times were rich in superstitious lore. Additionally, they were called "the inventions of the Devil," a phrase which reflected the Church's view of superstition in the Middle Ages. Many of these old superstitions have evolved into modern day customs (such as knocking on wood for good luck) in many parts of the world, including the United States, Europe and Great Britain.

Omens and superstitions often go hand-in-hand although they are actually two horses of very different colors. Omens are signs which, when properly interpreted, are believed to reveal the future, warn of impending danger, and so forth. Superstitions on the other hand are "beliefs in, or fears of, what is unknown, mysterious or supernatural." (The word "superstition" derives from the Latin *superstitio*, which means "excessive fear of the gods." The word "omen" comes from the Latin *ominosus*, meaning "foreboding evil.")

In this chapter you will find many of the herb-related superstitions and omens that exist in various parts of the world. Nearly all are rooted in antiquity and some continue to live on to this very day.

ALMOND

If you climb to the top of an almond tree, you can be sure of success in all of your business ventures.

You will find buried treasure if you carry almonds in your pocket. Almonds that are kept in a purse or pocket when the Moon is in a waxing phase will make your money increase.

Eating almonds is said to break fevers, increase wisdom, and even keep a person from becoming intoxicated when drinking alcohol.

ANGELICA

Angelica has been associated with angelic beings since early times. It was believed that the plant bloomed on or around the eighth day of May (the feast day of Saint Michael the Archangel in the old Julian calendar). According to one legend, an angel revealed in a dream that angelica would cure the plague.

Its common name is derived from *herba angelica*, which is medieval Latin, meaning "angelic plant."

Throughout the Dark Ages, angelica was used as an herbal amulet to ward off sorcerers and evil spirits and to break curses. It was named "the Root of the Holy Ghost" and was believed by many Renaissance doctors to be able to cure all maladies known to man.

ASH TREE

A child suffering from rupture can be cured by being passed through a split ash tree. Afterwards, the tree must be "plastered with loam and carefully swathed up."

Breaking a bough from an ash tree will bring you the greatest misfortune.

No serpent will ever lie in the shade of an ash tree, which (according to Welsh folklore) has a "spite against snakes."

The ash tree is a great force against poison and offers protection against sorcery and tempests.

BASIL

Basil leaves crushed between two bricks will magickally transform into scorpions, according to a curious old superstitious folk belief from the country of Belgium. (How this one came to be is a pure mystery.)

In ancient Greece and Rome, a belief existed that basil was an herb that grew only in the gardens of those who suffered misfortune or physical abuse.

BAY LAUREL

This tree has been, since ancient Roman times, believed to possess the power to guard against lightning strikes, sickness, Witches, the Devil, and bad luck.

When all the bay trees in a country withers, it is an omen that the king of that land will soon die.

It is bad luck to burn wood from a bay laurel tree.

BEAN BLOSSOMS

Sleeping in a beanfield all night will cause you to experience frightful nightmares. Some say that it can also lead to insanity.

When bean blossoms are in bloom, the chances of miners getting injured or killed while on the job are greatest.

When carried in the mouth, beans act as protective amulets against those who practice the arts of black magick.

BIRCH TREE

To protect a baby from being stolen by fairies and re-placed with an ugly changeling, place birch branches over the child's cradle or carriage.

Crossing your fingers while standing under a birch tree will protect you against all forms of sorcery.

In Russia, birch trees were believed to ward off the evil eye when red ribbons were tied around their stems.

BROOM

Broom brought into the house (especially in the month of May when it blossoms) will bring bad luck or death to the head of the family.

If a branch of green broom is used to whip a child, his or her growth will be permanently stunted.

CARAWAY

German folklore claims that a dish of caraway placed under a child's bed will offer him or her the greatest protection against sorcerers and all evil entities of the night.

Caraway placed in or on any object will make it invisible to thieves.

CLOVER

Finding a four-leaf clover brings exceptional good luck, riches, protection against sorcery, good health, a faithful lover, and the supernatural ability to see fairy-folk.

The legend of the lucky four-leaf clover, which is believed to have originated in the country of Ireland, is known throughout the world.

DAFFODIL

You will have bad luck for the rest of the year if the first daffodil you see in the Spring has its hanging head turned toward you.

Daffodils that are brought into the house will bring bad luck and keep geese, ducks, and chickens from laying eggs.

ELDER

Bad luck will surely come your way if you burn green elder. In parts of England, it was believed that doing so would invite the Devil to enter your house through the chimney.

Elder wood (also called "Witch-wood" or "wicked wood") will cause a fire in the fireplace to die out if placed upon it.

You must apologize three times to an elder when pruning it or cutting it down, otherwise bad luck will befall you.

A wound caused by an elder bush is fatal.

Furniture made of elder wood is unlucky, and elder sticks brought into the house will cause illness in the family and misfortune. A Danish superstition says that if you have furniture made from the wood of the elder tree in your home, you will be haunted by the dryad who lived in its branches.

Elder is said to ward off and cure disease. It offers protection against all forms of evil, saddle sores, and lightning; and its leaves repel hexes and curses when they are gathered on the last day of April and worn or carried as a charm.

To see elder in a dream is an omen of sickness in the near future.

FENNEL

Fennel hung over the doors and windows of your house on Midsummer's Eve will keep all evil spirits, sorcerers, demons, and the Devil at bay.

Fennel seeds placed in the keyholes of doors will also keep ghosts from entering a house, according to medieval superstition.

FERNS

If you cut ferns or throw them into a fire to burn, you will cause a rainstorm.

Some folks believe that ferns are extremely unlucky plants and call them "Devil's bushes," while others believe that ferns can protect against sorcerers and the Devil.

In the sixteenth century, it was a common belief that fern seed could give a person (especially a Witch or Wizard) mastery over invisibility. Another popular superstition from that era is that a fern gathered on Saint John's Eve and then placed in a shoe will enable a lady to attract a husband.

GOOSEBERRY

A thorn from a gooseberry bush will cause warts and sties to vanish, according to nineteenth-century Irish folklore.

In England at the turn of the eighteenth century, many children were led to believe that babies grew in the ground under gooseberry bushes and were dug up by doctors with golden spades.

GORSE

Never bring gorse (also known as "furze-flower") into your home, according to Victorian-era folklore from England. To do so will cause one of the members of the family to meet his or her death within the year.

In Wales, gorse hedges were planted around homes to keep them safe from mischievous fairies. It was believed that gorse had the power to repel all inhabitants of the fairy kingdom.

HAWTHORN

In Ireland it was believed by some that bad luck and the wrath of angry elves befalls those who dare to pluck a fairy hawthorn tree.

Cutting down a hawthorn causes grave illness or a death in the family.

Lightning never strikes a hawthorn tree, and if you nail a piece of hawthorn to your house on Holy Thursday, it will never be struck by a bolt of lightning. (This folk belief was popular in Normandy.)

If carried three times around an ancient hawthorn tree, a dying person will be made well again.

HEATHER

White heather is considered to be very lucky; however, all others are said to be just the opposite.

To bring heather into the house will cause a death in the

family (unless the heather is white).

Any tree that is planted within a circle of heather will be particularly fruitful.

If you burn heather, you will make it rain.

HOLLY

Holly berries were believed at one time to cure chilblains, and the branches of the plant were said to prevent fever, cure whooping cough, protect against lightning, and keep evil sorcerers at bay.

Cutting down a holly tree invites bad luck, as does sweeping out a chimney with holly. Bad luck is also said to befall those who do not have holly in their homes at Christmas.

HYDRANGEA

An old superstitious belief regarding hydrangea is that it will cause your daughters to forever remain spinsters if it is planted near your house (especially by the front door). This belief was popular in England in the early twentieth century.

Burning the bark of the hydrangea breaks the hex of any Witch or sorcerer.

IVY

The death of ivy that grows on the wall of a house presages the death of a member of the family who dwells within.

Ivy that is brought indoors will bring in bad luck, and if picked from the wall of a church, it will cause you or a loved one to suffer a grave illness in the near future.

Ivy should only be allowed in the house at Christmastime, and then nowhere else but in outer passages and doorways.

LETTUCE

Those who desire to have children should avoid lettuce at all cost, according to plant lore from the Middle Ages. If a man eats lettuce seed, he will become sterile, and a woman who grows lettuce in her garden will never be able to bear children.

LINDEN

A piece of linden bark wrapped in a spider's web and set beneath a green stone in a ring will guard a man or woman who wears it against the plague, according to a superstition from the Middle Ages.

In Europe, linden branches were hung over the front door to prevent evil from entering the home.

The linden is believed to be a tree of immortality, and those who carry its bark are protected against intoxication when drinking liquor.

MANDRAKE

A mandrake root will exorcise all evil energies, spirits, and demons from a house.

Uprooting a mandrake root from the earth is said to cure lumbago; however, it also curses the person who pulls it with the inability to have children. To hear a mandrake root shriek when it is being pulled from the ground will cause madness.

(For more superstitions associated with the mandrake, see chapter 6: "The Magickal Mandrake.")

MISTLETOE

It has been believed since ancient times that mistletoe protects against a number of things, including fire, sorcery, the Devil, evil spirits, lightning, poverty, and bad luck.

Mistletoe is an antidote for all poisons and can cure any disease when worn on a string around the neck. It promotes female fertility and makes unmarried women dream of their future husbands when placed underneath their pillows.

Kissing under the mistletoe at Christmastime brings good luck; however, if a woman fails to kiss a man under the mistletoe, she will remain unmarried for at least another year. Lovers who do not kiss each other when under the mistletoe will become foes before the year is over.

A house without mistletoe at Christmas is inviting bad luck.

MOONWORT

The moonwort possesses the power the break chains and unshoe horses that tread over it, according to European folklore from the Middle Ages.

For years, many superstitious people believed that a Witch could magickally open any locked door simply by putting some moonwort into the keyhole.

It is a lucky plant for all persons born under the astrological sign of Cancer (which is ruled by the Moon).

If moonwort is placed in a sealed box or bag when the Moon is in its waxing phase, it will produce silver by the time the Moon is full.

MUGWORT

Mugwort protects against poison, sunstroke, infection, enemies, venomous beasts, sorcery, elves, and the evil eye. When carried or worn in a shoe, it keeps travelers from growing weary. Mugwort is also reputed to cure women's diseases and consumption.

The sign of the cross must be made each time you pluck mugwort, otherwise you will be cursed with bad luck or ill health, according to Christian tradition.

MUSHROOMS

At one time it was a common belief throughout the country of Ireland that if any person should cast their eyes upon a mushroom, it would cause the mushroom to stop growing.

MYRTLE

Your home will be blessed with an abundance of love and harmony if myrtle grows on each side of your front door.

For good luck and a happy marriage, a bride should plant the piece of myrtle from her wedding bouquet in the garden of her new home.

Flowering myrtle is considered by many to be the luckiest plant in the world.

Myrtle grows well only if it is planted by a proud person or an unmarried woman, and to cut one down will bring unhappiness, misfortune, or divorce to your home.

You will dream about your future marriage mate if you sleep with a sprig of myrtle directly under your head.

NUTMEG

Carry nutmeg in your pocket and it will cure or prevent backache, boils, lumbago, and rheumatism.

Nutmeg is said to bring good luck, and in the mid-eighteenth century, it was believed that if a young maiden carried nutmeg in her pocket, she would end up marrying an old man.

OAK TREE

The oak tree protects mortals against evil, bewitchment, and the magickal power of fairies.

A worm found inside an oak apple (a large round gall sometimes found on oak leaves) is an omen of poverty.

In Europe it was believed that avenging deities dwelled within all oak trees; therefore, cutting one down for any reason was a sure way to bring on bad luck.

If you catch a falling oak leaf on the first day of Autumn, you will have good health throughout the entire Winter.

Numerous superstitious beliefs center around the acorn of the oak tree: Acorns protect a home against lightning strikes when placed in windows. An acorn planted in the dark of the Moon attracts riches, and carrying acorns increases fertility in both men and women, wards off all harm and illness, and ensures immortality.

ONION

Cut-up onions and onion peels are believed by some to attract bad luck when kept in the house.

Onions can heal the bites of dogs, cure toothaches, ward off illness, and even purify the air. If you leave a piece of onion on the windowsill, it will absorb all incoming germs.

According to Victorian-era folklore from England, if you rub the juice of an onion on your schoolmaster's cane, it will cause the cane to split in half when he strikes you with it.

If you toss an onion skin away, you toss away your prosperity. Onion skins should be burned instead (which is also said to attract wealth!).

If you throw an onion after a bride on her wedding day, it will ensure that she never weeps.

PARSLEY

In the medieval era, it was believed that parsley thrived only if it was planted by a woman (especially one who was pregnant) or by any person whose soul was wicked. A gardener who was good could still grow parsley but only if he planted the seeds on a Good Friday by the light of a rising Moon.

Planting four times as much parsley as needed was also recommended, due to the strange notion that parsley had to go to the Devil nine times before it was allowed to germinate. Sometimes it forgot to come back again.

According to Pennsylvania Dutch folklore, parsley planted too close to the house will cause a death in the family.

Where parsley grows in the garden, the mistress is the "master" of the house.

It is very unlucky to give away or to be given parsley. Bad luck also occurs when parsley is transplanted or when a stranger plants it in your garden.

Sowing parsley seed or picking some parsley from the garden will help make a woman conceive. However, in some parts of England, the folk belief was just the opposite—parsley prevents a pregnancy from occuring.

If a sprig of parsley is planted in a woman's vagina for twelve hours, she will begin to menstruate within twenty-four hours.

According to an old children's myth from seventeenth century England, babies (especially newborn girls) are born in parsley beds. They must be dug up with care and then wrapped in a clean, white blanket.

Parsley sown on any day of the year except Good Friday is said to invite the Angel of Death into your home.

PEONY

When worn on a necklace (often with coral and flint), the dried root of a peony protects sleeping women from the erotic night-demons known as incubi.

Peony roots were often worn by children to cure epilepsy or to facilitate the growth of their teeth.

When burned as an incense, dried peony will protect those who travel on water against stormy weather.

In some parts of the world, peony roots were strung together on necklaces which were then worn around the neck or placed over cradles to protect young children from the magick and mischief of fairies.

POTATO

In England a folk belief was popular in the nineteenth century that wearing or carrying a potato in one's pocket could cure rheumatism, presumably by drawing the uric acid from the patient's body into the potato, which then shrivels up and turns as hard as a stone.

ROSEMARY

The funerary custom of mourners carrying sprigs of rosemary which are later cast into the grave after the burial service has its roots in the ancient belief that rosemary makes the spirit rest in peace.

Rosemary protects against the plague and the Devil, and drives away evil ghosts and thieves from houses when hung over the doors and windows.

Wearing rosemary ensures good luck and success in matters of love, and when placed underneath the bed, it keeps the sleeper safe from nightmares and harm.

ROWAN TREE

The rowan tree has been associated with Witches since early times. Therefore, it is ironic that it is regarded in English folklore as a preservative against bewitchments as well as the evil eye and the wicked magick of elves.

Rowan branches hung over the door keeps a house safe from lightning. It is also carried on board ships to guard them against storms at sea, and placed over graves to keep the spirits of those buried below from becoming restless.

RUE

According to ancient Greek and Roman superstition, rue that has been stolen out of a neighbor's garden will grow better than rue that has been raised at home.

To cure a headache, place rue leaves on your forehead. To ward off future health problems, wear rue on a necklace.

Rue protects against hexes and hauntings, and it was eaten by the Romans of ancient times in order to avert the dreaded evil eye.

SAGE

Sage is believed to prolong life when it is planted in a garden. Another old belief about sage is that it prospers only for households where the wives are the rulers.

A young maiden will see her future marriage mate if she picks twelve sage leaves on Saint Mark's Day as the clock strikes the midday hour.

A medieval tradition claims that sage growing in the garden indicates the prosperity of the household.

SAINT JOHN'S WORT

Also known as "scare-devil," the Saint John's Wort is a highly magickal and potent plant which has, since early times, been used to protect against the Devil, evil, phantoms, hauntings, frightful visions, sorcery, and all forms of enchantment, as well as fire and thunderbolts.

In the country of Wales, it is customary for many folks to hang sprigs of Saint John's Wort over the doors of their houses on Saint John's Eve for "purification of the home."

If a soldier wears or carries Saint John's Wort, he will be invincible, according to an ancient legend.

SAVORY

There is an old folk belief of unknown origin that says that the herb known as summer savory increases the sexual desires of men and women; however, winter savory does just the opposite.

When carried or worn as an herbal amulet, summer savory is said to strengthen the powers of the mind.

SEAWEED

In many English fishing villages, pieces of dried seaweed (also known by the nickname of "lady's trees") are kept in the house, especially on the mantel above the fireplace, in the old belief that they have the power to keep the house safe from fire.

SPEEDWELL

Picking blue speedwell flowers will cause angry birds to peck out your eyeballs.

In certain parts of Yorkshire, England, an old belief existed that a child who gathers speedwell will cause his or her mother to die before the year is done.

TARRAGON

This herb has long been associated with mythical dragons and ancient serpent-goddesses.

In many parts of the world, it is believed that tarragon can cure the bites of snakes when it is eaten or rubbed on the wound.

THYME

According to superstition, a branch of wild thyme carried into the house of an old or ailing man will surely cause him to die. How or when this folk belief originated is a mystery.

If a young maiden wears a sprig of thyme in her hair, she will become irresistible to the opposite sex.

Carrying thyme as an herbal amulet gives a person courage, and wearing it enables one to see the fairy world.

VERVAIN

Vervain is one of the most magickal of all plants and has been the center of numerous folk beliefs since early times.

It protects against enemies, cures just about every disease known to man, wards off snakes, prevents nightmares, scares away the Devil, and enables an ordinary mortal to look into the future.

It has been used by various cultures around the world as a potent ingredient in love potions and as a plant amulet to dispel bad luck and attract good fortune.

According to Christian folklore, the bleeding wounds of Jesus Christ were miraculously healed with vervain.

VIOLET

In some rural parts of the United States, it is believed that violets are weakened by the sound of loud thunder. It is also said that thunder causes starlike spots to appear on the plant.

Violets have been used magickally to heal wounds and protect against wicked spirits.

Some believe that if you make a secret wish as you pick the first violet you see in the Spring, your wish will come true for you.

WOLFSBANE

In medieval Europe, it was believed that the flowering plant known as wolfsbane (or aconite) offered protection against werewolves and vampires when worn on a necklace or carried as a charm. To keep these bloodthirsty supernatural creatures from entering a house at night, wolfsbane (often along with garlic) would be hung over all doors and windows.

YARROW

Yarrow leaves placed inside the nose eases the pain of a migraine headache.

Plucking yarrow from the ground will cause your nose to bleed.

Yarrow brings good luck and offers a person protection against his or her enemies. It also averts evil spells and keeps bad Witches and demons from entering a house when strewn on the doorstep.

To ensure true love for at least seven years, a newlywed couple should hang a bunch of dried yarrow flowers over their bed.

Many folk healers throughout Europe and the United States still believe in the old wives' tale that claims baldness can be prevented by washing your hair with an infusion of yarrow.

YEW

The yew is a tree which has long been associated with death and funerals.

A yew brought into the house at Christmastime will cause a death to occur in the family before the year is over.

Branches of yew are cast into graves by mourners to make the spirit of the buried person rest in peace. However, medieval sorcerers and necromancers believed that yew (magickal potions and powders made from it) could bring the dead back to life.

12

A Wiccan Glossary of Herbalism Terms

Abortifacients: Botanicals which can induce the fatal and premature expulsion of an embryo or fetus from the womb. Angelica, juniper, mayapple, pennyroyal, rue, and tansy are examples of abortifacient herbs.

Alteratives: Botanicals which tend to favorably alter a condition and restore normal health. Alteratives are frequently combined with aromatics, bitter tonics, and demulcents: agrimony, American mandrake, American spikenard, bittersweet, black cohosh root, bloodroot, blue flag root, blue nettle root, dock, horseheal root, mayapple, pipsessewa, scabwort root, and speedwell.

Annual: Any plant that lives and grows for only one year or growing season, during which the life cycle (the germination of the seed through flowering and death) is completed. The following plants are classified as annuals: anise, basil, blessed thistle, borage, chervil, chickweed, cleavers, common groundsel, cornflower, cotton, eyebright, fenugreek, flax, fumitory, Herb Mercury, Herb Robert, horseweed, Indian tobacco, jimsonweed, knotweed, larkspur, marijuana, milk thistle, oats, pansy, plantains, prickly poppy, psyllium, pumpkin, red poppy, safflower, shepherd's purse, smartweed, star thistle, summer savory, white mustard, and wild thyme.

Antiasthmatics: Botanicals that are smoked or taken internally to relieve bronchial asthma: California gum plant leaves, daisy, nettle, red clover (ground blossoms), and yerba santa.

Antiseptics: Botanicals which destroy the microorganisms responsible for causing infection: blue gentian extract, costmary, dead nettle, dogwood bark, Egyptian onion, elder, eucalyptus leaves and oil, garlic, horseheal root, horseradish, indigo broom, oak bark, plantain, scabwort root, smooth sumac bark, violet, and Witch hazel.

Antispasmodics: Botanicals which prevent or relieve involuntary muscle spasms and cramps such as charley horses, epilepsy, and menstrual pain: blue cohosh, cajeput, passion vine, and Roman chamomile.

Aphrodisiacs: Plants that are said to stimulate the sex

organs and intensify sexual desire in men and women: elder, ginger, ginseng, hazel, jasmine, juniper, lavender, lemon verbena, lovage, mandrake root, serpentaria root, sundew, and yohimbe.

Aromatics: Fragrant herbs used in potpourris, sachets, oils, scented candles, perfumes, etc. The following herbs are classified as aromatics: acacia flowers, angelica root, anise seed, bugle, burdock, calamus root, caraway, cardamom seeds, cinnamon, clove, coriander, honeysuckle, lavender, lemon verbena, lilac blossoms, mace, mint leaves, nutmeg, orange blossoms and leaves, orris root, rosemary, rose petals, southernwood, Saint John's wort, sweet pea, violet, and wintergreen.

Astringents: Botanicals which cause contraction of the skin tissue: agrimony, alder bark, alum root, avens, bayberry (bark and roots), bearberry leaves, black alder bark, blackberry root, black birch leaves, black cohosh, bugle, costmary, dead nettle, dock, dogwood bark, eucalyptus oil, European birch bark, fluxweed, goldenrod, hawthorn berries, hepatica, holly berries and leaves, horseheal root, Jacob's ladder, manzanita leaves and fruits, oak bark, periwinkle, pipsissewa, potentilla, scabwort root, shepherd's purse, smooth sumac seed heads, southernwood, Saint John's wort, sweet fern, trailing arbutus, wax myrtle, white birch bark, wintergreen, Witch hazel, and yarrow.

Bane: A deadly herb that possesses poisonous properties. The term is often used in combination, as in "henbane," "wolfsbane," "baneberry," and so forth. Since early times, sorcerers in just about every culture around the world have been known to be clever in the forbidden art of poison-craft, and in the Middle Ages, Witches were said to have done away with their enemies and rivals with various herbal banes. The most popular magickal poisons were made with belladonna, hemlock, henbane, and mandrake.

Biennial: Any plant that completes its life cycle in two years or growing seasons. Most biennial plants normally generate leaf growth in the first year, and then bloom, produce fruit, and die in the second year. The following plants are classified as biennials: alkanet, caraway, celery, clary, dill, evening primrose, feverfew, foxglove, goat's beard, high mallow, hound's tongue, mullein, parsley, prickly lettuce, Queen Anne's lace, raspberry, red clover, rocket, scurvy grass, sweet clover, and teasel.

Bitter Tonics: Botanicals with a bitter taste which stimulate the flow of gastric juices and saliva, increase the appetite, and aid digestion: black haw bark, blessed thistle, bugle, dandelion, dogwood, goldenseal root, and wild cherry bark.

Carminatives: Botanicals which are used to induce the expulsion of gas from the stomach and intestines: cayenne pepper, dandelion, fennel, feverfew, ginger, parsley, peppermint, thyme, and yarrow.

Cathartics: Botanicals and other substances which cause evacuation of the bowels. Cathartics are divided into two categories: laxatives and purgatives. A laxative produces gentle bowel stimulation, while purgatives induce more forceful evacuation to relieve severe constipation. Laxatives: aloe vera, balmony, boneset, bunchberry, chicory, dandelion, dock, horehound, horseradish, hydrangea, magnolia, olive oil, red mulberry fruit, walnuts, and white ash bark. Purgatives: barberry, blue flag, castor oil, chaparral tea (or spurge), fennel, mayapple, poinciana leaves, and senna leaves.

Corrective: A term used by herbalists to mean an herb

that is added to food or medicine to improve the taste or smell of it.

Decoction: A medicinal or magickal extract made by adding herbs to boiling water (normally one ounce of dried herb to one pint of water) and then allowing the mixture to simmer for usually thirty minutes.

Demulcents: Herbal substances taken internally which soften and smooth inflamed mucous membranes and are used to treat coughs and minor throat irritations: blessed thistle, borage, coltsfoot, goldenseal root, hound's tongue, and Solomon's seal.

Diaphoretics: Herbal substances taken internally to increase sweating. Such substances are also called sudorifics, and are frequently used to break common colds and fevers and to promote good health: black cohosh, broom, cajeput, calendula, catnip, chamomile, elder flowers, garlic, ginger root, horseheal, hyssop, Jacob's ladder, linden flowers, mugwort, oregano, pennyroyal, rosebay, saffron, salad burnet, scabwort, serpentaria root, vervain, and yarrow.

Diuretics: Plants which increase urine secretion and work to correct urinary disorders: agrimony, balm, bearberry, black cohosh, blue cohosh, blue flag, boneset, broom, chicory, cleavers, cucumber seeds, daphne bark and root, garlic, germander, gravel root, ground cedar, horseheal, horseradish, horsetails, hydrangea, joe-pye weed, juniper berries, parsley, pipsissewa, pumpkin seeds, rosebay, rue, scabwort, shepherd's purse, sorrel, sunflower seeds, vervain, wild carrot, wood sage, wormwood, and yarrow.

Emetics: Plants which induce vomiting: adder's tongue, bay, black mustard seeds, blue flag, bloodroot, cliffrose, elkweed roots, hedge-hyssop, ilex berries, mandrake, mayapple, wake-robin roots, and white mustard seeds.

Expectorants: Botanicals which loosen phlegm of the mucous membranes and promote its expulsion: benzoin, bloodroot, chokecherry, coltsfoot, garlic, horehound leaves, licorice root, slippery elm bark, storax tree bark gum, sunflower seeds, sweet gum, vervain, violet, white pine (dried inner bark), and yerba santa leaves.

Green Healing: *See* Green Witch

Green Magick: *See* Green Witch

Green Witch: A nickname for a female or male Witch who is skilled in the art of wortcunning. The herb magick practiced by a Green Witch is called "the Green Arts" or "Green Magick"; the use of medicinal herbs is known as "Green Healing."

Herb: The dictionary defines an herb as "a fleshy-stemmed plant that generally dies back at the end of each growing season" or "any plant or plant part used specifically in medicine or as seasoning." Herbs are mainly thought of as the green leaves of any plant or tree (both fresh and dried) that is valued for its medicinal, savory, or aromatic qualities. Although many herb books regard seeds, roots, flowers, berries, and bark as herbs, they are more accurately classified as spices. Trees also do not come under the technical heading of an herb; however, tree leaves and some shrubs are considered to be herbs by many.

Herbal: A book about herbs and plants, especially those which possess medicinal and healing properties (based on scientific evidence) or those whose medicinal values are based entirely or in part on conjecture or folklore. One of the most interesting and popular herbals of all time is Nicholas Culpepper's astrologically influenced herbal guidebook entitled *The English Physician* (also called *The Complete Herbal*). It was originally published in the mid-seventeenth century and remains popular in modern times, especially among Witches and students of herbalism and plant lore.

Herbalism: The practice of identifying and using plants or plant parts that are: aromatic, savory, and medicinal. A man or woman who grows, collects, or specializes in the use of herbs (especially those that are used medicinally) is called an herbalist. The study of herbs is known as herbology.

Herbalist: *See* Herbalism

Infusion: An infusion is a medicinal or magickal fluid made by pouring boiling water over one or more herbs (usually one cup of water to every teaspoon of dried herb) and allowing the mixture to steep like a tea, usually for ten to fifteen minutes, in order to extract the soluble elements and active principles.

Perennial: Any plant that has a life span longer than two years. The following plants are classified as perennials: agrimony, alfalfa, aloe, American ginseng, angelica, autumn crocus, balm, bay, belladonna, bindweed, birthroot, bistort, black cohosh, bladderwrack, bloodroot, blue cohosh, blue flag, boneset, buckbean, bugleweed, butterfly weed, California poppy, catnip, celandine, chamomile, chicory, chives, cinquefoil, colicroot, coltsfoot, comfrey, daffodil, dandelion, dog rose, elecampane, fairywand, fennel, figwort, fireweed, forget-me-not, garden (or salad) burnet, garlic, goldenrod, goldenseal, Good King Henry, gromwell, ground ivy, heal-all, hops, horehound, hyssop, lady's mantle, lady's slipper, lavender, lily of the vally, live-forever, liverleaf, loosestrife, lovage, maidenhair fern, marjoram, marsh mallow, mayapple, meadowsweet, milkweed, mints, moneywort, moonseed, motherwort, mouse-ear, mugwort, onion, oregano, Oswego tea, partridgeberry, passionflower, pipsissewa, pussytoes, rosemary, rue, sage, Saint John's wort, Sampson's snakeroot, skullcap, Solomon's seal, sorrel, speedwell, spikenard, stinging nettle, stoneroot, sundew, sweet flag, sweet woodruff, tansy, tarragon, thyme, vervain, Virginia snakeroot, wallflower, watercress, water lilies, wild ginger, wild senna, wild strawberry, wild thyme, wild yam, winter cress, wintergreen, winter savory, wood sorrel, wormwood, woundwort, yarrow, and yellow flag.

Philtre: An herbal aphrodisiac used in magickal spells with incantations to arouse love or sexual desire. Also known as "love potions," philtres have been used by Witches since ancient times and have consisted of many different herbal ingredients. They are often put in foods or drinks and work the best when prepared and used on a Friday (the day of the week most sacred to Venus, the ancient goddess of love) or at the time of the month when the Moon is positioned in the astrological sign of Taurus.

Phytotherapy: The treatment of illness by the use of herbs or medicinal substances which are derived from plants. Witches refer to this art as "Green Healing" and have practiced it for centuries.

Potion: An herbal tea or brew used by Witches in magickal or healing rituals. In order to work properly, a potion must be prepared during the appropriate phase of the Moon and made with herbal ingredients possessing the correct magickal properties. Potions are traditionally brewed in cauldrons and are used in all facets of the magickal arts. Potions concocted for the workings of love magick are often called "philtres."

Poultice: Herbs mixed with hot water (or a pastelike herbal medicine) that is heated, spread on a cloth or towel, and then applied to an inflamed or painful body part in order to warm, moisten, or stimulate. Poultices are also used by herb doctors for drawing out infection and foreign bodies as well as for relieving muscle spasms.

Sedatives: Herbs which sooth, calm nervousness, and tranquilize: bugleweed, catnip, chamomile, fennel, heal-all, hop vine oil, horsebalm, Linden flowers, New Jersey tea, passion vine, scullcap, skunk cabbage root, valerian, viburnum, and Witch hazel.

Simple: This is an archaic word used by Witches of old to mean a plant of medicine or the medicine obtained from it. Simples, which are a mainstay of many folk healers and country Witches, are usually very mild and indigenous plants. They arc uscd completely by themselves to prevent or treat disease.

Soporifics: Botanicals which are used to induce sleep: barberry, bay, catnip, chicory, goldenseal, hops, lavender, lemon balm, lemon verbena, onion, passionflower, Saint John's wort, sweet woodruff, and valerian.

Stimulants: Herbs which increase or speed up the various functional actions of the human body: angelica, bayberry bark and roots, black pepper, bloodroot, calendula, caraway, cayenne pepper, coriander, elder flowers, garlic, horseheal root, horseradish, lavender, mayweed, nettle, nutmeg, pennyroyal, pine, prickly ash bark, rosebay, sassafras root, scabwort root, serpentaria root, sweet flag, vervain, wild ginger, wintergreen, wormwood, and yarrow.

Stomachic: Plants which have curative properties in easing disorders of the stomach: angelica, avens, blessed thistle, blue gentian, bogbean, burdock leaves, cayenne pepper, elecampane, ginseng, gum plant, hop plant, lemon verbena, oyster plant, peppermint, Roman chamomile, rosemary, salsify, spearmint, sweet flag, and yerba buena.

Suffumigations: Magickal incenses made from herbs and burned by Witches and magicians to attract spirits and enable them to materialize. Suffumigations are used in ceremonial magick, seances, and necromancy. Anise, dried carnation flowers, dittany of Crete, frankincense, dried gardenia petals, heather, pipsissewa, sweetgrass, and wormwood are the herbs most commonly used by Witches as suffumigations.

Tincture: An herbal medicine that is made by mixing four ounces of powdered or finely cut herb with one pint of spirits (such as brandy, gin, or vodka). The mixture is kept in a large, tightly sealed jar for about two weeks and shaken several times daily to enable the medicinal properties of the herb to be released into the alcohol. After the two-week period, the tincture is then strained through a cheesecloth into another clean bottle and stored until needed.

Tonics: Plants which strengthen or invigorate the body and stimulate general health: agrimony, avens, barberries, bayberry bark and roots, bloodroot, burdock, chamomile, chicory, coltsfoot, dandelion, ginger, goldenrod, horehound, Joe-pye weed, mint, pipsissewa, red clover, rue, sea holly, selfheal, speedwell, sweet fern, sweet flag, tansy, vervain, watercress, Witch hazel, wood sage, wormwood, and yarrow.

Unction: The act of anointing a person or ritual tool with an herbal ointment or oil as part of a consecration, magickal ceremony, or healing ritual. Unctions are commonly performed in the spells and rituals of Wicca Craft. The term "unction" is also used for a balm, oil, or salve.

Unguent: A special ointment or salve used by Witches to promote healing and to induce astral projections and psychic dreams. Also known as flying ointment and sorcerer's grease. In the Middle Ages, unguents containing various hallucinogenic ingredients were believed to give a Witch the powers of flight, invisibility, and transformation.

Vulnerary: Herbs which are used to treat minor external wounds such as burns, cuts, and scrapes: all-heal, comfrey, horsetail grass, marsh mallow root, and plantain.

Witch-Draught: In medieval Witchcraft and sorcery, a Witch's potion, brew, or philtre made from various herbs believed to possess magickal properties and used to control or manipulate the emotions or thoughts of others.

Wort: A word stemming from the Old English *wyrt*, meaning a plant or herb. It is used chiefly in combination: mugwort and Saint John's wort are two examples.

Wortcunning: The knowledge and use of the secret healing and magickal properties of herbs; a word used by folk healers, Witches, and Wiccans of all traditions to mean the practice of herbalism. Wortcunning has been associated with the Old Religion since ancient times.

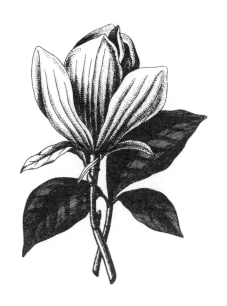

13

Resources

Abyss Distribution
48 Chester Rd. (Dept. WIG)
Chester, MA 01011
(413) 623-2155
(Fax) (413) 623-2156
Free occult catalogue! Over 2,400 books, plus 5,000 other
ritual items. Amulets, jewelry, herbs, perfumes, incense,
burners, candles, statues, and more. Magickal one-stop
shopping. Retail and wholesale.

Golden Isis
P.O. Box 525
Fort Covington, NY 12937
Publisher of *Golden Isis* magazine (ISSN 1068-2457), a quarterly newsletter/journal of Goddess-inspired poetry, Pagan art, Wiccan news, book reviews, ads, and more. Sample copy: $2.95; one-year subscription: $10 (Canada and overseas: $15). Also from Golden Isis: Tarot and Gypsy-Witch card readings, reasonably priced natal charts, past-life readings, dream interpretations, spell-casting services, *Circle of Shadows* by Gerina Dunwich, and much more! Please send a self-addressed stamped envelope for more information.

Gypsy Heaven
115 G South Main St.
New Hope, PA 18938
(215) 862-5251
Gypsy Heaven offers a wonderful catalogue of books, music, amulets and talismans, incense, oils, herbs, God and Goddess statues, crystal balls, and their own line of spell candles and spell kits. Catalogue: $3.00 (refundable).

Joan Teresa Power Products
P.O. Box 442
Mars Hill, NC 28754
(704) 689-5739
Large selection of hard-to-find herbs and roots. Some plants available, shipped live from their nursery. Also oils, incenses, books, etc. Free catalogue.

Marah
P.O. Box 948
Madison, NJ 07940
Learn magical herbalism and make incenses to enhance your rituals with Marah's *The Magic of Herbs*, $29.95

postpaid. Full line of Wiccan herbs also available, plus flower oils, handcrafted incenses, candles, books, Wicca course, and other enchantments. Send $1.00 for catalogue, incense sample, and free issue of *Marah's Almanac*.

The Sage Garden
P.O. Box 144
Payette, ID 83661
(208) 454-2026
Herbs, common and hard-to-find essential oils, spell kits, amulets, talismans, garb, statuary, runes, unique anointing oils, filler-free incenses, bath and beauty items, and jewelry. Publisher of WPPA member publication *Artemesia's Magick!* Other services include tarot readings and custom orders. Catalogue: free with large self-addressed envelope and three stamps.

Shadow Enterprises
P.O. Box 18094
Columbus, OH 43218
(614) 262-1175
Shadow Enterprises offers a unique collection of one-of-a-kind items, fine metaphysical supplies, ritual tools, jewelry, new, used, and rare books, collectibles, book search service, and much more. For more information, send $1.00 to the above address, or if you are in the Columbus area, you may visit their catalogue showroom, *The Shadow Realm*, located at 21 West Brighton Road.

Shell's Mystical Oils
P.O. Box 691646
Stockton, CA 95269-1646
Shell's is happy to bring to you their new catalogue with a larger line of herbs due to popular demand. Top-of-the-line tinctures, sprinkling powders, incenses, and oils. Catalogue: $2.00.

White Light Pentacles/Sacred Spirit Products
P.O. Box 8163
Salem, MA 01971-8163
This company is dedicated to the propagation of the Wiccan arts and magickal sciences. They are the distributors of thousands of authentic spiritual tools, talismans, jewelry, and supplies, plus many other offerings for the celebration of life. Cast a mighty spell in your home or office! Blessed be! Catalogue: $3.00.

Bibliography

Boxer, Arabella, and Philippa Back. *The Herb Book*. London: Octopus Books, 1980.

Bulfinch, Thomas. *Bulfinch's Mythology*. New York: Dell, 1967.

Crockett, James Underwood, Ogden Tanner, and the editors of Time-Life Books. *Herbs*. Alexandria, Va.: Time-Life Books, 1977.

Cunningham, Scott. *Cunningham's Encyclopedia of Magical Herbs*. St. Paul Minn.: Llewellyn Publications, 1985.

Davidson, H. R. Ellis. *Gods and Myths of Northern Europe*. Harmondsworth, England: Penguin, 1964; reprint edition, 1986.

Dietz, Marjorie J., ed. (originally edited by F. F. Rockwell). *Ten Thousand Garden Questions Answered by Twenty Experts*, 4th ed. Garden City, N.Y.: Doubleday, 1982.

Dunwich, Gerina. *Candlelight Spells*. New York: Citadel Press, 1988.

_____. *The Concise Lexicon of the Occult*. New York: Citadel Press, 1990.

_____. *The Magick of Candleburning*. New York: Citadel Press, 1989.

_____. *The Secrets of Love Magick*. New York: Citadel Press, 1992.

_____. *Wicca Craft*. New York: Citadel Press, 1991.

_____. *The Wicca Spellbook*. New York: Citadel Press, 1994.

Farrar, Janet, and Stewart Farrar. *Eight Sabbats for Witches*. Custer, Wash.: Phoenix, 1981.

Fox, Helen Morgenthau. *Gardening With Herbs for Flavor and Fragrance*. New York: Macmillan, 1940.

Gabriel, Ingrid. *Herb Identifier and Handbook*. New York: Sterling, 1979.

Garland, Sarah. *The Herb Garden.* New York: Viking Penguin, 1984.

Guiley, Rosemary Ellen. *The Encyclopedia of Witches and Witchcraft.* New York: Facts on File, 1989.

————. *Harper's Encyclopedia of Mystical and Paranormal Experience.* New York: Harper San Francisco, a division of Harper Collins, 1991.

Hamilton, Edith. *Mythology.* Boston: Little, Brown, 1942.

Harris, Ben Charles. *Better Health With Culinary Herbs.* New York: Weathervane Books, 1971.

Hayes, Elizabeth S. *Spices and Herbs Around the World.* Garden City, N.Y.: Doubleday, 1961.

Hylton, William H., ed. *The Rodale Herb Book.* Emmaus, Pa.: Rodale Press, 1974.

Kowalchik, Claire, and William H. Hylton, eds. *Rodale's Illustrated Encyclopedia of Herbs.* Emmaus, Pa.: Rodale Press, 1987.

LaBarre, Weston. *The Peyote Cult.* New York: Schocken Books, 1969.

Llewellyn's 1995 Magical Almanac. St. Paul, Minn.: Llewellyn Publications, 1994.

Lorie, Peter. *Superstitions.* New York: Simon and Schuster, 1992.

Magic and Medicine of Plants. Pleasantville, N.Y.: Reader's Digest Association, 1986.

Miller, Richard Alan. *The Magical and Ritual Use of Herbs.* Rochester, Vt.: Destiny Books, 1993.

Muir, Ada. *Healing Herbs and Health Foods of the Zodiac.* St. Paul, Minn.: Llewellyn Publications, 1993.

Opie, Iona, and Moira Tatem. *A Dictionary of Superstitions.* Oxford, England: Oxford University Press, 1989.

Parker, Derek, and Julia Parker. *The Compleat Astrologer's Love Signs.* New York: Grosset and Dunlap, 1974.

Pepper, Elizabeth, and John Wilcock, eds. *The Witches' Almanac, Aries 1994–Pisces 1995.* Milton, Mass.: Pentacle Press, 1994.

Phillips, Roger, and Nicky Foy. *The Random House Book of Herbs.* New York: Random House, 1990.

Richardson, P. Mick. *Flowering Plants (Magic in Bloom).* New York: Chelsea House Publishers, 1986.

Robbins, Rossell Hope. *The Encyclopedia of Witchcraft and Demonology.* New York: Bonanza Books, 1981.

Saneck, Kay N. *The Book of Herbs.* Secaucus, N.J.: Chartwell Books, 1985.

Shaudys, Phyllis. *The Pleasure of Herbs.* Pownal, Vt.: Storey Communications, 1986.

Thomas, Pamela. *Growing and Cooking With Herbs.* New York: Crescent Books, 1991.

Walker, Jane. *Creative Cooking With Spices.* Secaucus, N.J.: Chartwell Books, 1985.

Wedeck, Harry E. *A Treasury of Witchcraft.* Avenel, N.J.: Gramercy Books, 1961.

Westland, Pamela. *The Herb Handbook.* New York: Gallery Books, 1991.

Index

192